Do You Talk That At Home?

How to write copy that sounds less like drivel, more like a conversation

<u>JAMES DANIEL</u>

To George & Andrea, & all @Inspire

Now you know my best-kept secrets – use them wisely!

James Daniel

Earth Monkey

First published in Great Britain in 2013
By EarthMonkey Media Ltd:
Sandringham House
1-3 Cemetery Road
Bridgend
CF31 1LY

Text © James Daniel 2013

The moral right of James Daniel
to be identified as author of
this work has been asserted.

All rights reserved. No part of this publication may be reproduced in any form or by any electronic or mechanical means including information storage and retrieval systems, without the prior permission of EarthMonkey Media Ltd.

ISBN 978-0-9567442-1-0

A catalogue record for this book is available from the British Library.

Printed and bound in Great Britain by
www.printandpublish.co.uk

Cover design by www.springcreative.co.uk

This book has been written to offer authoritative information on the subject matter. Neither the publisher nor the author is engaged in providing you with specific advice in relation to your business. You must therefore use your own discretion when acting on the information herein, or otherwise seek individual support from a professional service provider.

**To Mrs Canton, Miss Veryard
and Mrs Whiteman**

*You were fabulous English teachers...but if you
ever read this, you'll gnash your teeth
and curse my name 'til doomsday!*

Contents

INTRODUCTION

The evils of corporate chaff.................12
A vital lesson learned from a man who hid behind boardroom waffle

PART 1:
BREAKING THE HABIT

1 – Your natural voice........................24
Teasing out the way you talk 'til it's out there on the page

2 – Clarity first...................................43
The perils of witticisms, wordplay and other ambiguous hoo-hah

3– Grammar? Sometimes....................55
Getting on the wrong side of your old English Teacher

4 - Beware the uber sentence.............65
How to say it all, without saying it all at once

5 - Let it flow....................................77
Because making a point is more than throwing in random facts

PART 2:
WHO'S READING THIS ANYWAY?

6 – Your language - or theirs?..............90
A bit of mirroring now, just for good measure

7 – What's eating Phil?......................102
Finding buttons to push, before you start pushing

8 – Starting the conversation............112
Writing headlines that grab attention...WITHOUT SCREAMING AT THE READER!!!

9 - The You Factor............................128
For every reader asking "What's In It For Me?"

PART 3:
TAKING SHAPE

10 - Sales letter structures................142
Non-pushy ways to write and fill your order book

11 - Sales letter pitfalls.....................157
A few caveats before your message hits the mat

12–Writing to inform........................180
Staying on the radar with regular content

AND FINALLY

Final word: getting started................202

"If you talk to a man in a language he understands, that goes to his head. If you talk to him in his language, that goes to his heart."

Nelson Mandela

Points of order

Firstly, thank you for reading this. Most books just sit in the Amazon warehouse or on lonely bookshop shelves. Even the lucky few that find a loving home will just sit in the "some day" pile, and most go un-thumbed for years on end. So I'm truly humbled that you're giving this your attention. Thank you.

Now, before we dive in, I want to stress a couple of things:

"Copy" means everything you write to promote your business

OK you probably don't need a definition, but just to be clear - it's anything and everything you write, for any media.

A sales letter needs copy. So does a web page, an email, a brochure, a press release, a flyer, an advert, an article, a video script...basically, if it uses words, we'll call it copy.

Of course, I don't know what type of copy you'll be writing. You might be writing to inform your readers, or to spur them into action. I couldn't say - so in my bid to please one and all, I've tried to cover a few different bases.

Part One of this book covers the basic steps of conversational writing. Whatever your message or media, you can apply this stuff to good effect.

Part Two looks at who you're writing to, and how to make sure your message fits.

Finally, Part Three looks at angles and structures for different types of copy: sales copy using the classic AIDA principle, then factual content like reports, articles and blog posts. I've also added a chapter here on direct marketing. It's going slightly off-topic, I know, but I hope it will give you some thoughts on how to put all this stuff into practice.

This is a guide for people who have to write copy...but not for copywriters!

If you're a copywriter (well, a good copywriter) you should tut at this book with a smug little grin and say "Tell me something I don't know". That's because you already know about keeping it light and personal.

You know how to turn features into benefits, how to structure a message, how to simplify long sentences...you've heard it all before.

And while this book gives my thoughts on how to do it well, it's mostly Copy 101. If you're an expert, you'll start to nod off!

But if you're someone who has to write copy on the side, this book is for you.

You might be a marketing pro working with a small budget, so little luxuries like copywriters are a stretch too far. Or you're a business owner who sells, makes tea and does everything in between. Or you're an exec in some other field, who has to write now and then.

I'm guessing you'll be one of those things. Or at least, I hope so - because it's written with you in mind.

My examples ain't real
Mostly, where I've used examples, I've created a fictional setting. I might say "Suppose you're a mortgage broker, with a new 5 year fixed interest rate for first time buyers". Or "Let's say you're a Health & Safety Consultant helping businesses to cope with new *Safety At Work* legislation". Or whatever.

Please don't get caught up in the circumstances I describe, because they're all invented and used for illustration only. I only say this because I can't reply to emails asking how to get this great mortgage deal, or telling me why Health & Safety legislation wouldn't specify this and that. It's irrelevant.

Male equals male or female
I've used the male gender throughout this book wherever the text calls for a him, her, he or she. I had to choose male or female, so ever the pragmatist I flipped a coin and the boys came up tops.

Of course, you're welcome to get sidetracked by taking offence and writing me angry letters. But for the record, at least 50% of my clients and suppliers are women, as is 100% of the person I'm married to. Nothing divisive here.

If you want to blame someone or something, you could blame the English language for not offering a gender neutral pronoun. Apart from "it"...which opens up a big new can of worms.

Finally...maybe I'm wrong
This book is my take on how to write effectively. I've based it on my 25 years as a pro writer, including the last 8 years working solely as a copywriter and trainer. In that time, I've written for nigh on 200 companies and shared my tactics at conferences and seminars around the UK. So if this stuff didn't work, I guess I'd have starved to death by now.

That said, I can't guarantee you success. In fact if I could, this book would be a licence to print money and I'd be charging you seven figures, minimum:)

The point being, there are very few absolute rights and wrongs, and I'd be arrogant to the max if I claimed to have the ultimate answer. I don't. I can only share what works for me and draw on the best practice that's been developed by generations of awesome copywriters.

So yes, I'm fixed in my belief that conversational copy beats the waffly corporate alternative. But if you find otherwise *through genuine systematic testing* I'd be thrilled to hear about it. I'll even share it on my blog.

Just email james@jamesthecopywriter.co.uk with the subject line "Waffle works".

Mind you, I won't hold my breath. Because conversational *is* best!

**James Daniel
November 2013**

Introduction:
The evils of corporate chaff
A vital lesson learned from a man who hid behind boardroom waffle

---

Steve had been promoted - and no-one could tell you why. Just between us, he barely had the talent to answer the phone and hold a simple conversation. And yet, here he was, rising through the ranks of a growing UK corporation, and already overseeing a dozen call centres.

It should never have happened.

But it had. So he got to swan around, making big decisions and drinking in his own self-importance. And if anyone challenged his edicts, he had the perfect answer:

Big words.

No substance, no insight, no wisdom, but lots of "professional" sounding words and hackneyed phrases that he inflicted on anyone who'd listen. "Modus Operandi", "Temporal Factors", "User Centricity"...an endless stream of chaff that he bandied about like a membership card. His proof that he'd joined the club.

As you can imagine, he was fun to work with!

He didn't review things. Oh no, he preferred to "digest and inwardly scope" them.

He never used things – he only "utilised".

And I swear by this holy keyboard I'm tapping, he once promised to time some process or other with the pledge "I'll have it stopwatched".

It's true.

"I'll have it stopwatched".

But come on, no-one talks like that! Not in the real world (where "stopwatch" is a noun, Steve. A noun. Not a sodding verb!)

OK, I know there are Steves all over who hide behind that stuff at work, but it's not the real them, is it? They can't be like that all day long?

I must say, I was curious. So one day, I asked the question.

Chatting with Steve (if you can have a chat with someone who calls it a "pow-wow") he told me that he "fully endorsed" some new policy or other. I seized my chance:

"Tell me, Steve", I queried, "do you talk like that at home? You know, when your mum asks if you want spaghetti hoops for tea? Do you say 'Yes, I endorse that', or just go with 'Yum, sounds good to me'?"

Steve looked confused for a moment, then replied: "I don't live with my mum".

Mmmm.

Could have been worse, I suppose. He could have said "I've vacated the central family unit", so at least he'd drawn the line somewhere.

But I hope my point got across.

In our real selves, we'd never use the artificial language that festers in the boardroom. As soon as we get home and slip off the corporate mask, we see business speak for what it is: cold, pompous, distant and totally insincere.

Certainly not the kind of language to win over hearts and minds.

So for the love of whatever you worship, I'm begging you - don't use it!

Don't use it when you talk, because trust me you'll just sound like Steve.

And never, ever use it when you're writing copy.

Please!!

Time and again, split tests have shown that a casual, semi-formal message beats the pants off stiff and corporate.

And here are some good reasons why:

Reason #1:
People are emotional, not clinical
Take a look at this mission statement from a supermarket in the US:

> Guided by relentless focus on our five imperatives, we will constantly strive to implement the critical initiatives required to achieve our vision. In doing this, we will deliver operational excellence in every corner of the company and meet or exceed our commitments to the many constituencies we serve. All of our long-term strategies and short-term actions will be moulded by a set of core values that are shared by each and every associate.

Can you believe that was written by someone with a beating heart?

There's no emotion! It's like someone took a vacuum cleaner and sucked out all the emotive phrases. Only the cold and clinical words have survived the devastation.

It would be bad enough if they only used it internally...but no, this is out there on their website for real customers to read.

And that's a problem, because we as humans like to buy from other humans! We want to know, like and trust someone before we'll hand over our cash...and you'll never know or like or trust the someone who talks like a robot.

On the other hand, consider the warm, dulcet tones of natural speech. Imagine a message where "imperatives" are simply "things that matter", and people serve people - not "constituencies".

It could happen! Hold a normal conversation, where you share your feelings and personality, and you'll get to the heart of your prospect.

Know, Like and Trust are going to follow.

Reason #2:
Literacy standards are shocking!
Here in the UK, our average reading age is around 9-11 years. Maybe that's a reflection of a failing system, or the impact of endless telly, or a figure swayed by people who speak English as a second language...I don't know.

But I do know this - you can't ignore it. Whoever you're selling to.

In mass markets like retail, entertainment and leisure, your choice of language will kill or cure you. And even in B2b, it's a very brave bear indeed who assumes that every prospect can read beyond *Janet and John*.

So your best bet: keep it simple. The people who know all the big words will still understand the little ones.

Reason #3:
Make it a chore and no-one will read
Yep, scary but true. The person who glances at your copy isn't obliged to read on. It's your job to pull them in – so if reading is one big sweaty effort, you're going to lose them quickly.

It's one reason why copy is so different from other forms of writing.

Just think: you've bought this book - I hope - so chances are you'll stay with me even if the odd word doesn't resonate. And it's a similar tale with a newspaper or anything else you've paid for - you'll give each article a fair hearing, to make sure you get your money's worth.

But copy - especially sales copy - is a different beast. The reader knows full well that behind it all, someone wants to grab their cash. So their commitment is frail.

One bump in the road and they're gone. Out of sight. Bye bye.

Put those three reasons together and hopefully you can see the massive danger of talking to someone – anyone – in an alien voice!

So has the corporate world got it wrong?
No. Or at least, not entirely! Look at Virgin, or Disney, or Google and a small gaggle of others. When they write to businesses or consumers, they use a natural style.

But the rest? Yes, they've got it horribly wrong. I'll go on record and say, if you do the corporate thingyjig, you're losing money and business.

So why do people do it?

I don't know...but I could guess.

First, the wrong writing style gets beaten into us all from an early age. In school, we're taught to write formal letters, using passive language in the third person – instead of the active, first person language we all use in reality.

And second, at work we're all drawn into the myth of pseudo-professionalism: the idea that chatty language will undermine the company image, so it's as naughty as ripping off your suit and dancing naked round the car park.

Those two forces have left us dazed and confused, not knowing what to believe. So we follow the herd and we make the same old mistakes as everyone else.

"Ah yes James, but well no, you see..."
OK, since you've read this far, I hope you're already with me in principle. But some people, they do whine and moan and dig their pointy heels in. So in case you're there in the doubters camp, let's take a peek at some objections:

"Ah yes James, but...it's dumbing down, isn't it?"
Thanks for asking. No it's not.

Conversational copy is not about simplifying, or bending to the lowest common denominator. It's about holding onto the substance, and losing the fluff that surrounds it.

In fact, if anything, it's a way to *guarantee* substance. All too often, waffle is used as a veil...so when you pull the message apart, you can see there's nothing behind it.

But if you write without the fluff, well there's no hiding place. The quality of your content is exposed - so you'll make sure your plain old words are worthy of attention!

"Ah yes James, but...my customers are different"
Well yeah, but mostly no. See, they'll have their own quirks...priorities, buzzwords, little things that make them who they are. But (correct me if I'm wrong) they're all still human beings.

Correct?

They could be CEOs in the City, or specialist docs on Harley Street, or Cabinet Ministers, Diplomats, Presidents, Popes or whatever.

It makes no odds.

They're all shaved monkeys underneath, just like the rest of us.

Maybe you put them on a pedestal, but that says more about you than them.

They're just people, who blow off and eat pie and chips and watch Ant & Dec on Saturdays. They're just like you – and they'll respond to the same easy, chatty approach.

"Ah yes James, but...we have our own language, you see"
Yes, if you're B2b or serving a small consumer niche, I'm sure your tribe has its own hatful of words and phrases. That's great. That's all good bonding stuff, and it helps to tell your customers that you're one of the gang.

But what about the words *around* the buzz words? Here's a rule of thumb:

> [chatty] [buzz] [chatty]
> beats
> [waffle] [buzz] [waffle]!

So do it, use the vernacular...but you don't have to dress it up. If you were out hob-nobbing at some industry bash, you'd keep it real bar the jargon.

Just do the same in writing. It's all I'm asking, y'know.

Rant over.

Now, if you hadn't twigged yet, that's what this book is about.

As a freelance Copywriter, I've written in umpteen styles for clients across the board. Some selling products, others services. Some high end, some bargain basement. Some B2b, some B2c...and it's never made a difference.

I've always had my best results with casual, easy copy that mirrors the way we all speak out in the real world.

Sure, I might vary the tone...being a tad more formal for Daily Mail types, and slack as you like for the tabloid set...but still, it's just conversation.

So, in the coming chapters, we're going to break the habit of formal writing so you can keep it all nice 'n' simple.

We'll look at all kinds of tactics, but there's only one principle here:

If you wouldn't say it, don't write it.

If in doubt, remember the spaghetti hoops...

PART 1
BREAKING THE HABIT

"How people keep correcting us when we are young! There is always some bad habit or other they tell us we ought to get over. Yet most bad habits are tools to help us through life."

Jack Nicklaus

– 1 –
Your natural voice
*Teasing out the way you talk
'til it's out there on the page*

To kick things off, let's try creating a mini business profile - a quick overview that just says who you can help, and how.

But don't agonise too much over the actual content. Right now, our focus is not *what you say*...it's all about *how you say it*. We want to turn your copy into a written version of your natural voice.

And there's an easy way to get started:

Forget that you're writing!
It really is that simple. For some reason, we all start to panic the second we grab a pen. Maybe it triggers memories of exams or English lessons, when anything less than formal would get you a big red mark and a scowl off Miss? I don't know the reasons. But still, 90-something percent of us struggle to put our natural voice down on paper.

So just for a moment, forget about writing. Chat to a friend and say what you want to say...record the conversation...and when you transcribe it, you'll be amazed. Even if you don't have the finished message, you won't be miles away.

Another way to drop "writing anxiety" is to charge headlong at the page. Set a stopwatch, alarm or timer and give yourself 5 or 10 minutes to write in free flow. No stopping, no edits, no scribbles – just write the words as they spill from your mind.

You might find it helps to do this when you're most relaxed – say after a bath or a mini snifter of your favourite tipple. Or curl up on the sofa with a notepad. Whatever works for you. There are no rules – although I doubt you'll do your best work wearing a collar and tie, because that'll throw you back into formal work mode.

Above all though, don't panic if you struggle at the first attempt. Formal writing can be a hard habit to break, so try one or both exercises a few times over until you've written about 200 words that feel like a part of you.

That's your mission.
Do it now before you read the next bit.

Done it? Good stuff – it means you've got something you can work with!

We'll call it your *practice message*. And we'll keep referring back to it, so keep it somewhere handy.

Now let's go back and edit...applying some of these principles to make it a little more *you*:

Make it personal

Your message might be read by hundreds or thousands (maybe millions) of people. But you're not addressing them all - you're only addressing one person. He's sitting at home in his favourite armchair chewing over your letter. Or at the office, hunched over his desk and checking out your web page. Or at the bus stop, roaming through mobile sites or flicking through emails.

Just you to him...but multiplied by hundreds or thousands.

Every TV and radio presenter on earth has had this lesson drummed in. In their world, the cardinal sin is saying "Hello everyone", or "If any of you know the answer" or anything else that gives the idea of talking to a crowd. You'd never say that one-to-one, so you wouldn't say it on air.

Use the same principle in everything you write, and you'll sound far more natural.

Here are two other ways to keep it personal:

Don't be a We when you can be an I
People deal with people – not brands or companies. So wherever possible, address the reader as you the person, not you the corporation.

In other words, "I'm sure you'll agree" beats "we're sure you'll agree".

It's a simple change that works wonders. Hearing from you (the senior figure) as an individual tells the reader you care and you'll take ownership – not like the faceless company where problems can get swallowed up in the system.

This touch is especially important in personal media like letters and emails, where the message is traditionally from one person to another.

But even in corporate media, like web pages and brochures, there are opportunities to add a personal voice.

You could give an intro statement, as the person behind the brand. You could act as a guide or narrator all the way through the message. Or you could pop up here and there, with advice or recommendations...plenty of chances to be an "I". "We" is the last resort.

Don't be super-human
There are self-appointed and wannabe gurus who talk down to their readers. Their sub-text is "You're an idiot, but I'm amazing so shut up and listen!"

Not good. Sit in an ivory tower, and the people will pelt you with stones. But if you trade as one of the people...if you admit to mistakes and frailties...you'll be lavished with love and riches.

Well, you know. Maybe.

Quick example: in one video on my website, I talk about the things I can't do. I'm a DIY disaster, I can't cook or run or kick a ball. So don't hire me to paint your shed, because you'll be hugely disappointed. But hire me as a writer...well yeah, I guess I can do that.

Clients tell me they respect my honesty – and because I'm not the Big I Am, they're quicker to believe me when I promise to solve a marketing problem.

By the way: this might sound like it's only for the one-man business, but larger brands can profit from self-deprecation too. Admit mistakes, apologise, show how lessons are learned....it all makes you human and more attractive as a business.

Use positive language
Language brings ideas to life. Even if something happened in the past, or hasn't happened yet, your phrasing can breathe life into the message. Here are some ways to do it...

Be active, not passive
"Active", if you don't know, means focusing on the subject, while "passive" means focusing on the object. Take this example:

> [PASSIVE]
> A great time was had by all
>
> [ACTIVE]
> We all had a great time

The subject is "We" or "all". The object is "a great time".

Let's put this another, non-classroomy way. In the active version, we're focusing on people doing things, while in the passive, we're looking at things being done by people.

It's a vital difference, because passive language dulls the edge of the copy...so somehow (don't ask me why) it feels less important. Less alive.

It's very easy to break this habit, but it's also easy to fall back into the old ways. (Yep, I'm sure you'll find accidental passives in this book). So keep an eye out for lapses.

Just for good measure, here are some more examples of passive Vs active:

- ☒ It will be done today
- ☑ I'll do it today

- ☒ The copy will need to be rewritten
- ☑ You'll need to rewrite the copy

- ☒ Carbohydrates should be avoided
- ☑ You should avoid carbohydrates

- ☒ A new way of writing has been discovered
- ☑ We discovered a new way of writing

I'm sure you get the idea...start with a person doing something and you can't go wrong.

Choose positive words (well, usually)
Most of the time, your copy should use upbeat, positive words. Examples being "yes", "can", "will", "do", "always", "create", "master", "make", "result", "win", "easy", "believe",

"more"... and others like that. Used well, they give your message a happy, smiley feel.

Generally, you want to avoid the negatives. Words like "not", "no", "but", "can't", "won't", "don't", "never", "hard", "impossible", "barrier", "obstacle", "block", "stop"...all those whinging, problem-heavy words that just weigh your message down.

There are semi-negatives too. Words that undermine you, like "if", "maybe", "might", "could", "would", "perhaps", "doubt", "consider", "try", "unsure", "uncertain" and more. They can burden your message as much as any negative.

Staying upbeat is wise, most of the time. Even if it's not *the natural you* (for all I know, you're a miserable git) it pays to show your sunnier side if you want to win hearts and minds.

But there is a note of caution: the negs and semi-negs work well in some situations.

Rule of thumb, if you're describing a problem, ladle the negs on with a big spoon. Then once you're describing a solution, go for happy-clappy talk.

Don't neglect to avoid pointless negatives
(It's ok, that's deliberately vague - you'll see why in a moment...)

As we've just said, negatives have their place - but they should be handled with care. As well as negging the reader out, they can cause confusion.

So if you can, spin negatives into positives - as in these examples:

- ☒ I'm not going out today
- ☑ I'm staying in today

- ☒ It won't be done until tomorrow
- ☑ It will be done by tomorrow

- ☒ I'm not saying I can't be there
- ☑ I can be there

- ☒ I'm not saying I can't not be there
- ☑ I can give it a miss

In the first two examples, we're just taking a single negative and turning it on its head. That's easy enough - say your glass is half full and your statement becomes more appealing.

But the last two take it further, confusing the reader with double and triple negs.

"I'm not saying I can't be there" is a classic double negative. You have to unravel the thread to see how they cancel each other out.

And "I'm not saying I can't not be there" takes it to the extreme: we've got three negs in a row here. It would take a Forensic Linguist (if such a person existed) to fight through the layers of meaning and come out the other side!

Advice: keep it simple. Find all the negative statements and see if you can swap them for something more optimistic.

Use simple words
Take another look at that heading: "Use simple words". It's about as straight forward as you can get, and it gets the point across.

But I could have gone OTT and replaced "use" with "utilise". Instead of "simple", I could have said "unadorned". And instead of "words", well what about "lexicon"?

Utilise an unadorned lexicon

....mmm.

Why bother? The simple version gets the meaning across to every kind of reader, and the wordy alternative is just a wee bit crap.

Now I'm not going to get back on the soapbox here and rant some more about whys and wherefores. I'll just say this:

- Don't utilise when you can use
- Don't eliminate when you can get rid
- Don't facilitate when you can help
- Don't indicate when you can show
- Don't substantiate when you can prove
- Don't procure when you can buy
- And don't finalise – or terminate – when you can end or finish!

The list of long words Vs short could go on forever, but you should get the idea. "Optimum" is just a big word for "best", "maximum" for "most" and so on.

If you're used to using longer words, sorry – you've got some cold turkey ahead. In time, you'll beat the habit outright, but in the early days, review every message and keep asking "is there an easier way to say this?"

Dip into the common phrasebook
Phases are a big part of our shared vocabulary. They can help you sound more natural and improve the flow of your message.

Just beware: stick to colloquialisms...and steer clear of clichés.

Colloquialisms, if you don't know, are warm and familiar phrases. Think "easy pickings", "spitting distance", "keeping watch" and more. Used sparingly, they'll help you out – probably for two reasons:

First, we know the phrase instantly. We can process it that much faster, so it acts as a mental shortcut. Easy reading, no effort involved.

And secondly, it's familiar – which means it's pre-approved. It helps to break down resistance to the message overall.

Clichés, on the other hand, are nasty little things that tell the reader you don't care – about them or about your business.

Example: take this (genuine) piece I lifted from an online business coach:

> If you're hell bent on success, I can maximise your potential. I've been there, done that and bought the T-shirt, so let's turn your business into an awesome cash generating monster.

Uurrgghhhh!

Quite apart from the loathsome bullish hype and endless ego inflation, it's riddled with clichés – including the all time classic "bought the T-shirt".

Don't do it.

Repeating a cliché is nothing short of insane!

But strangely, toying with one can be a useful ploy. So you could use part of it, but stop short of the whole shebang.

Here's an example, for a taxi firm:

> [IFFY]
> Just pick up the phone and order. We'll be there in two shakes of a duck's tail.
>
> [ACCEPTABLE]
> Just pick up the phone and order. We'll be there in two shakes.

The result is an easy, casual phrase that stops short of naff 'n' corny.

OK, so what is and isn't naff?

Ah, the burning question! The thing is, it's a moving feast, because language and culture evolve. So today's harmless colloquialism can be tomorrow's evil cliché.

It also varies from reader to reader. Take our taxi example, where we need a phrase for "we'll be there shortly". Our phrase "in two shakes" would go down well with an older audience – and so would "on the double", "in a jiffy" or even "half a mo". But for a younger, cynical market, they're all super-corny! A slacker phrase like "soon as" would be a better choice.

So sorry, there's no such thing as a definitive guide on this. You'll have to make your own judgement:

Does it sound natural, coming from you? And how will your readers respond?

There's a whole load more on appealing to the reader later on...

Don't oversay it
Bad habits can sneak back when you let down your guard. So check your copy for *overwriting*. These rules will give you a hand:

Use simple structures
We've already seen the absurd phrase "utilise an unadorned lexicon". And now, if you're ready for this, there's an even worse alternative.

How about:

> Adopt the utilisation of an unadorned lexicon

That's about as ridiculous as the English language can get...but it happens! Mostly in public sector policy docs, but still – it's vile and it's out there.

It's a technique known as nominalisation – the largely pointless act of taking a verb and turning it into a noun. So "substantiate" becomes "substantiation", "finalise" becomes "finalisation" etc.

Nominalisations give us two problems. Firstly, they're even more OTT than their opposite numbers in the verb list...and secondly, they lead to awkward and ham-fisted structures. Instead of a simple word like "use" (or its nasty brother "utilise"), we get "utilisation of". As in:

> [IFFY]
> We need to promote utilisation of the new website
>
> [ACCEPTABLE]
> We need to get people using the new website

It's a no brainer, innit? Why tie yourself up in knots?

Use contractions
Compare these two sentences:

> [IFFY]
> I am not saying it is the best cafe in town. But they are open, so let us give it a try.

> [ACCEPTABLE]
> I'm not saying it's the best cafe in town. But they're open, so let's give it a try.

The first version sounds stilted and unnatural, because it leaves out the contractions – the shorter versions of words that we all use when we talk.

Of course, there are times when you need to use the full version, like "I will not" rather than "I won't" – especially if you're making a strong statement by drawing attention to the longer phrase.

Example:

> I will not be able to make the same offer again this year

...is more resolute than:

> I won't be able to make the same offer again this year

Generally though, if you're striving for casual, contractions win hands down.

And finally...the sanity check
Hopefully you've reviewed your Practice Message now, with amends and scribbles a-plenty. But before we toddle off to the next bit, here are two last things to chew on:

Be consistent
The real you is coming through...but don't let it slip. Your language has to be consistent all the way through your message. Take your eye off the ball, and you might find the odd stray word creeping in.

Here's an example from a home cleaning firm:

> If you want us to work on one room and leave others alone, we will. If you want us to work on furniture, or windows, or worktops, we will. After all, it's your home, so we'll deliver your target outcomes.

D'oh! It was all going so well until "deliver your target outcomes". A simple, easy read, focused on the needs of the customer...then the corporate speak worms its way in.

A nice colloquialism would have worked better. Something like "It's your home, so you call the shots".

Same point, more chatty.

Consistent!

Read it out loud
Once you've written your copy, read it back – out loud, not in your head. And be honest: how does it sound?

Could you use the same words in a conversation?

If not, highlight all the words and phrases that sound odd or stilted, then go back and make some changes.

And so on, 'til it all sounds like you.

Summing up
Finding your natural voice can be the hardest part of the process. You might have to unlearn everything you've been told up 'til now, and start seeing the written word in a different light.

So if you have to, staple this mantra to the wall of your office:

Copy is not about taking language to some higher plane. It's about holding up a mirror, with the words we all use every day.

Once you've made this breakthrough, and written a page or two of natural sounding copy, take a moment to jump for joy - you're over the biggest hurdle!

From here on in, we're just tweaking.

Next stop, clarity...

AT A GLANCE

- ✓ Forget that you're writing
- ✓ Don't be a 'We' when you can be an 'I'
- ✓ Be humble, not super-human
- ✓ Use positive language
- ✓ Be active, not passive
- ✓ Don't forget not to use double negatives
- ✓ Use simple words
- ✓ Use common phrases...but be wary of clichés
- ✓ Use simple structures
- ✓ Use contractions
- ✓ Be consistent
- ✓ Then read it out loud...is it you?

You're not learning a new skill.
Just forgetting one that gets in the way.

– 2 –
Clarity first
The perils of witticisms, wordplay and other ambiguous hoo-hah

---

Copywriters should be more Alan Sugar than Oscar Wilde. Straight talking beats seven bells out of being a Clever Trevor. You need to be as clear – even as blunt – as you can be.

If you've studied other forms of writing, you might struggle to get your head around this. Dramatists, for example, thrive on sub-text that alludes to hidden or deep-seated meanings – so the big faux-pas in their world is writing a line of exposition that feels obvious or "on the nose".

But in copywriting, that's a luxury.

Your audience doesn't have the time or inclination to play guessing games. Remember, you have to draw them into your message, and if it's a chore they won't bother.

So in this chapter, we'll look at some golden rules for keeping it clear and simple.

Avoid witticisms

One of the worst adverts I've ever seen came from a national chain of opticians.

The ad showed a pic of some glasses, with this headline:

> So your eyes won't envy your ears

I've read it a thousand times over now, and I've got to admit, I still don't get it.

> So your eyes won't envy your ears

What does it mean? Please, someone give me a clue! Really...if you get it, then please email james@jamesthecopywriter.co.uk and tell me what I'm missing!!

But let's say someone does get it. How will they respond? There's no benefit there, no reason to buy...so the best the ad can hope for is "Ha ha, how terribly witty".

And that might scoop the ad agency a nice award or twelve, but I'll eat my bestest hat if it's sold a single pair of goggles.

In contrast, try a benefit statement like "20% off designer sunglasses". It might not be clever or sexy, and it won't win a single award. But it will make money because it's compelling and unambiguous.

Kerching.

Avoid wordplay
In my distant youth, I spent 2 years selling cable TV door to door. On my first day, the boss showed me a new flyer he was ever so proud of. The company had launched a new package called "The Choices". So the copy ran:

> The Choices
> (Yours)

Nothing else. Just that and a phone number.

"Great, isn't it?" he asked.

"Um, I don't get it", said I.

"Well, the choices – that's the package. And the choice is yours, because you can choose."

By this time he was looking at me like I was an imbecile, and no doubt wondering if there was a get-out clause in my contract. But I persevered:

"Does the person reading this know we have a package called The Choices?"

"Don't know. Probably not."

"So it wouldn't mean anything to them?"

"Oh right, I see what you mean. But you know, some will know about it."

"So for those people, what are we saying?"

"Well we're telling them about The Choices."

"But they already know. We're not saying anything new."

"Yes but we're reminding them, aren't we?"

"Kind of. But why don't we tell them why it's so good - say what's in it for them?"

"Oh I don't know. Look don't worry, it's gone to print now anyway."

So I was stuck with it. Working door to door, using collateral that meant a big fat nothing to nobody. Thankfully, it was ditched soon after, but for two weeks the reaction on the doorstep was emphatic.

"What are you talking about?"

"I don't get it"

"What the hell is this?"

See, we made it an effort – a big cryptic puzzle – and people don't want to be guessing.

So please, oh pretty please, keep puns and wordplay out of your copy!

"OK, but tell me this JD...why is wordplay doomed to failure?"
I'm glad you asked. Take a look at this image. It's a famous optical illusion that you've probably seen online a thousand times before.

Some people see a wineglass. Others see two people standing face to face. And eventually, most people see both, fading quickly from one to the other.

But no-one ever sees both at once.

Puns work the same way. You might get both meanings, but one will come first and the other lags behind. And there's no way to control which way round the penny drops.

Let's take this headline that I lifted from an insurance company's advert:

> We'll insure you never have to worry again

It's a play on words, between "insure" and "ensure" – and like the illusion here, it has two meanings built in:

1. We'll insure you (so that) you never have to worry again
2. We'll ensure (make sure) that you never have to worry again

When you read the headline, you have to infer – in other words, process the message and decide for yourself what it means. Your mind will probably select either version 1 or version 2 as a default, the same way as you'll either see the faces or the wine glass first.

Then, a split second later, you might see the second meaning – so you'll understand it's a play on words, and focus your mental energy on reconciling the two different meanings. The same way that you stare in fascination at the changing image.

But that's mental energy wasted. Energy you could have given to processing a benefit statement and imagining the peace of mind you'll get from said insurance.

And it gets worse.

You might only understand one of the two versions – so you miss half the meaning anyway.

Or you might fail to see the built-in meanings altogether – so you just see the words on the page, and wonder why the grammar and spelling don't make sense!

Cor, it's a right old mess, innit?

Either it leaves you bewildered, or you get the pun...but you're focusing on the wordplay, not the proposition.

So either way, it's failed!

Now, you might think this is nit-picking, but it's really not. You want your message to hit the emotional part of the brain that drives decisions – but wordplay re-routes the message to the part of the brain that's reserved for language.

In sales terms, that's like ignoring the decision-maker and pitching your wares to the family dog!

Not wise. Not wise at all.

And last...avoid careless slips
Witticisms and wordplay are deliberately vague. But sometimes, ambiguity comes from careless phrasing. Two meanings pop up, and all for want of some well-placed words or punctuation.

Careless Slip #1: The Dodgy Pronoun
Take this example:

> The boss advised the new guy to buy his lunch from the canteen

"His" could mean boss or new guy. So take it out and all becomes clear. As in:

> The boss advised the new guy to buy lunch from the canteen

Another problem could happen with plurals. As in:

> The boss advised each of the new guys to buy his lunch from the canteen

Greedy boss? Not when you say this:

> The boss advised each of the new guys to buy their lunch from the canteen

Or drop the pronoun again. As in:

> The boss advised each of the new guys to buy lunch from the canteen

Simples.

Careless Slip #2: The Iffy Adverb
Have a look at this:

> Reading normally improves the mind

Hmm. Does reading in a normal way improve the mind...or is it normal for reading to improve the mind?

Now I don't know what reading in an abnormal way is. So let's assume it means the latter. Then it would be better to say:

> Normally, reading improves the mind

Or better still, consider what we mean by "normally" and replace it with a more suitable word. Maybe:

> Regular reading improves the mind

Or:

> Reading usually improves the mind

...whichever meaning is intended.

Careless Slip #3: Missing Punctuation
To finish, here's an old classic you might have seen.

Consider:

> A woman without her man is nothing

Compared with:

> A woman. Without her, man is nothing.

Punctuation can change the whole meaning of a sentence in one fell swoop, so make sure it's working for you – not against you. Remember:

> Use punctuation well before it damages your message

And:

> Use punctuation well, before it damages your message

Summing up

If you were stuck on a desert island, writing a message in the sand, you'd want to keep it short, punchy and unambiguous. "SOS" does the job perfectly well...so you wouldn't get clever and spell out a teasing "Wish You Were Here" instead!

You just couldn't take the risk of being ignored or misunderstood.

Well whatever your message, your business really is on a desert island – and screaming out to the planes overhead. You can't afford ambiguities, because there's just too much at stake.

Whether you mean to be vague or not, a lack of clarity will kill the message. So keep the deliberate clever stuff at arm's length and keep an eye out for ambiguous slip-ups.

AT A GLANCE

- ✓ Don't be witty or clever: you need sales, not awards
- ✓ Avoid wordplay: it only confuses
- ✓ Make sure pronouns refer to one person or group or thing – not two
- ✓ Make sure adverbs relate to just one part of the sentence
- ✓ Use punctuation carefully. It can help or undermine you
- ✓ If in doubt, ask someone else: is it clear to them?

Careless words won't cost lives...
but they'll cost you a ton of business

– 3 –
Grammar? Sometimes
Getting on the wrong side of your old English Teacher

True story: a copywriter (not me) was hired by a business woman to write a direct mail piece. He sent off his copy, then two days later he got this reply:

"My daughter studied English at university and she's corrected your grammar."

The copywriter rattled off a quick response. It said:

"If only your daughter had studied Marketing. Then she might have known better!"

OK, so he gets zero out of ten for customer relations. But he did make a valid point.

Our mission is to write in a way that's easily understood – and when grammar supports that, whoop-de-doo. But when it doesn't, we have to ignore it.

Correct English and acceptable English are very different things.

So the next step in developing your natural writing style is knowing when to use grammar, and when to push it aside.

Don't be a Grammar Nazi
Here's a paragraph that fails the grammar test on a few technicalities:

> Long story short. I did turn up, but I still thought we were meeting at yours. But by the time Jack told me you'd rearranged, I was already on your doorstep. And it was raining, and I was wet through, and feeling like rubbish anyway...I just couldn't face the long walk into town. Really sorry about that. It's not something I'm proud of.

Even without knowing the background, it's easy to understand that this is someone explaining why they didn't meet their friend in town. It's simple and conversational – but English Teachers and other Grammar Nazis would jump on all kinds of "mistakes".

I'm not going to give a definitive list here, so no emails on this one please...but here are some of the errors that would be picked up:

- "Long story short": Grammar Nazi says "You can't make a sentence without a verb"

- "But by the time...": Grammar Nazi says "Starting a sentence with the word 'but' is forbidden"
- "And it was raining": Grammar Nazi says "Starting a sentence with the word 'and' is forbidden"
- ", and I was wet through": Grammar Nazi says "Using the word 'and' after a comma is forbidden"
- "I just couldn't face": Grammar Nazi says "Contractions are improper. This should read 'could not'"
- "Really sorry about that": Grammar Nazi says "This is another sentence without a verb"
- "Something I'm proud of": Grammar Nazi says "Prepositions should not fall at the end of a sentence"
- And so on, 'til the whole paragraph is covered in big red circles

But back in the real world, none of that matters one bit...

- The occasional ultra short sentence can work. With or without a verb!
- "But" can start a sentence
- "And" can start a sentence too, and come straight after a comma

- It's fine to use contractions. "It is fine to use contractions" sounds odd
- Prepositions can end a sentence. It's something we'll all put up with...
- Contractions are only natural, like we've said already

So now let's see the version that gets the Grammar Nazi's approval:

> For the sake of brevity, I shall condense my version of events. I arrived as appointed, but still holding the original belief that we intended to meet each other at your residence. However, by the time that Jack had informed me of your decision to re-arrange our meeting location, I had completed my initial journey. At this point, the rain had commenced and thus my clothing was wet. Moreover, I began to experience a sense of nausea. Consequently, I did not relish the prospect of a lengthy walk into the town centre. I apologise for missing our appointment. May I assure you that this is not a matter of which I am proud.

Now if you want to sound like Noel Cowerd standing in a witness box, be my guest. It might get you through an exam, but it won't put your message across.

"OK...but do you have to break the rules?"
No, of course not! Do what you want...there's no have to, there's only what works. It's just that breaking a few rules will help your message along because it makes you sound more human, less robotic.

The big example is using "and" at the start of a sentence. It speeds up the flow, instantly connecting one idea to the next - and it does it more succinctly than "Moreover", "In addition" or any other conjunction.

That's why we do it. And if Teech has a coronary, so be it. The world won't implode and you'll get your point across...he's just collateral damage!

Okey-doke, so that's one side of the story. Now here comes the flip side:

Be a Grammar Nazi sometimes!
For all the spleen venting of the last section, there are bits of grammar that should never be flouted, not in a gazillion years.

Apostrophe crimes for one
Put an apostrophe in the wrong place and you'll confuse your readers. Plus, about 1 in 4 readers (me included) will chase you to the gates of hell brandishing a large apostrophe-shaped stick.

So yeah, that's one to avoid.

The most common apostrophe sin has to be the dreaded plural. Don't ask me why, but some folk have unilaterally decided that the letter "S" can't end a word unless it's buddied with an apostrophe.

They seem to think it's a rule, like the weird Q and U thing.

Oddly though, there are two factions: some who think the apostrophe belongs before the "S", and some who think it goes after.

Just to be clear here – its neither.

The apostrophe doesn't form plurals! You don't use it in "people", "children", "sheep" or "dice", so why inflict it on "carrots"?

Think I'll stop there, because I'm getting cross now.

There are other crimes against apostrophes (like the classic "who's" Vs "whose") but let's not get into that here. The rule is, apostrophes are used to show possession or contractions. Google something like "rules for apostrophes" if you're not sure what's what.

Just as long as we're clear – this is one part of grammar you shouldn't ignore!!

Then there's spelling
Misspelling is a definite no-no. It slows down the read, and it angers many. So keep an eye out. Spellcheckers ain't perfect.

In particular, watch out for homophones – words that you could liken to non-identical twins, like "allowed" and "aloud", "meet" and "meat", "pact" and "packed" or "two" and "too". Use the wrong version and your spellchecker will be none the wiser. And even your grammar checker can be duped.

Type in "the radio's aloud in here" and "the radio's allowed in here"...you'll see what I mean.

Be vigilant.

And finally there's structure
Grammar comes into its own when it dictates structure. Deep seated in the structure of any sentence, there are no-go areas that stop you from changing the order of words or adding words that don't fit.

Example: take a simple sentence like "Pass me the salt please". Grammar won't allow erratic re-ordering, as in "Pass please the salt me".

And it won't allow random new words, as in "Pass me butter the salt please".

Not to get technical, but these variations are obviously wrong to us because grammar is hard-wired to our neural pathways - and when a sentence veers off course, it creates a jolt in our minds.

Now I know you're not going to throw random words like "butter" into your copy, but that's an extreme example, just to make a point. In practice, this becomes an issue in more subtle cases. A small word here and there that squats illegally in a sentence, and your reader won't process your copy as easily as they should.

Example: compare these two sentences:

> [VERSION A]
> This is something everyone should try, at least once
>
> [VERSION B]
> This is something where everyone should try it, at least once

In Version B, the words "where" and "it" are out of place. Yes, it's a teeny-tiny difference, and we can still make sense of it. But the error confuses the reader – even if it's just for a micro-second.

Result: the copy isn't flowing smoothly and seductively. Instead it's moving in fits and starts. And sorry, but that ain't persuasive!

Summing up

Don't throw grammar out of the window. Get rid of the pernickety stuff that spoils communication, but keep the rules that help you to get your point across.

If you're not convinced – and you think grammar should never be flouted - think on:

The most successful sales letter ever written promoted a subscription offer for the Wall Street Journal.

Written by the late copywriter Martin Conroy, it ran continuously - beating test after test - from 1974 'til 2002. In that time, it brought in a massive $2.5 billion in sales.

The letter does all the things we've been talking about here. It willingly breaks the pedantic rules, but follows the important ones.

So just for fun, I tested it at grammaryly.com – arguably the best automated grammar checker on the web.

The results say it all:

A grammar rating of 49%. And a verdict that says (I kid you not!) "weak, in need of revision".

Puts it all in perspective, don't ya think?

Don't let grammar stand in your way!

AT A GLANCE

- ✓ Is anything unclear? Any word, or phrase, or paragraph?
- ✓ Would it make more sense if you relaxed the grammar grip?
- ✓ OR have you gone too far? Do you need to rein it in? Have you taken liberties with spelling and punctuation?

Let grammar help you when it helps you...and drop it when it hinders

– 4 –
Beware the uber sentence
*How to say it all, without
saying it all at once*

Long sentences can kill your copy. Researchers say the best length is around 14 words. At 25 words, the reader starts to struggle...and once you hit 40 words, all hell breaks loose in their mind! They lose their thread and forget where they started.

So it's always best to split a long sentence into two or three.

That doesn't mean that every sentence should be ultra-short or identical in length. It would get boring very quickly if they all took the same form.

Better to think of it like a tennis match...if every shot is identical, it will send you to sleep. But when the players mix it up, they add a bit of variety – mixing volleys with baseline attacks and overhead smashes. It varies the pace.

So your job is to break down the uber sentence, then build it up again with a more solid structure.

Take this example, lifted from a web page selling skincare products:

> There are no added chemicals in this handmade soap, because additives can aggravate the skin or cause rashes, especially if you have sensitive skin, but thankfully this product is different so you can use it every day.

Like most long sentences, this is trying to say too much too quickly. It feels like an over-excited 5 year old rattling off a Christmas list without pausing for breath. It witters on with no sense of direction, repeating and going back on itself.

As a result, you can barely keep tabs on it. Message lost.

So let's start breaking it down by listing the main points:

- Handmade soap
- No added chemicals
- No rashes or aggravation
- Safe for sensitive skin
- Safe for everyday use

So far so good. Now we can start over...

We'll start with the two main points the reader needs to know – the features:

> This soap is handmade and free of chemicals.

Then we can move onto the consequences – or benefits:

> So even if your skin is sensitive, you can use it every day. No rashes, no aggravation.

So now the whole thing reads:

> This soap is handmade and free of chemicals. So even if your skin is sensitive, you can use it every day. No rashes, no aggravation.

Now don't get me wrong, I'm not claiming this is the greatest piece of copy ever written! But this time, it makes sense because the info comes in the right order and we've lost the bits we didn't need.

Here are some other things to look for when you break down the uber sentence:

Kill embedded clauses
If you don't know, an embedded clause, like this, is a sentence (or partial sentence) inside

another sentence. Or to put it another way, a confusing interruption.

Take this example:

> I'm looking forward to meeting my new boss Mike Jessop, who's joining us from JBM Enterprises, when he starts on Monday

The main sentence is:

> I'm looking forward to meeting my new boss Mike Jessop, when he starts on Monday

Simple enough. But the meaning is confused when we add in:

> who's joining us from JBM Enterprises

So it would be better to say:

> I'm looking forward to meeting my new boss on Monday. His name's Mike Jessop - he's joining us from JBM Enterprises.

The original version is messy, because your brain has to stop and start as you try to make sense of it. But the alternative lets you process one piece of information at a time.

Drop redundant words
Imagine that you've got a tiny space, so word count is as tight as can be. Do you really need every word that you use in the sentence?

Probably not.

Let's look at that first line again. How about:

Imagine you've got a tiny space, so word count is tight. Do you need every word?

We've just saved 12 words, and the meaning hasn't changed! Because while the original wasn't awful, it was overblown. In particular:

- ..."Really" adds nothing. It's as meaningless and bland as "nice" or "lots".
- ..."That" just gets in the way. "Which" often does the same.
- ...And there's no need to over-qualify, as in "every word that you use in the sentence". The last three words are just filling space. Like saying "It's invisible, so you can't see it!"

Use Synonyms
Even when your sentence is whittled down from uber to bijou, you'll still find one nagging little pest. It's called repetition.

The same word needs to appear twice...and the second time, it sounds careless and clunky.

That's where synonyms come in. As in this example:

> I've worked for the same company for 25 years. It's a great company to work for.

As opposed to:

> I've worked for the same company for 25 years. It's a great business to be part of.

"Company" and "work" have been replaced in the second half of version two, so the message flows more easily. Just a simple change that makes a big difference.

Finding synonyms is easy enough. As you'll know, Word and other packages offer a thesaurus - and there are thousands of online tools with the same power or more. Just one warning: any tool will offer you big words as well as small. So remember the goal is writing in the same easy way that you talk.

Bullet it
Bullet points make your copy more accessible. No secret there. With bullets, it's easier to scan the message and pick out the most important info.

And that's a great alternative to the uber sentence, because:

- Every point has room to breathe
- Sentences needn't be complete – so you can drop boring functional words
- There's no limit to your bullet list – so you can break down an ultra-long sentence

When you're writing bullets, the most important rule is consistency. Every bullet should read as a natural follow-on from your intro statement. As in this example...

> This product will help you to:
> - Do this
> - Do that
> - Do the other

Far too many bullet lists ignore this basic rule. They use stray bullets that come in from all directions. As in:

> This product will help you to:
> - Do this
> - You can also do that
> - Thanks to new technology, you can do the other

See the difference? The reader will still know what you're driving at, but now the seamless flow has been broken.

One easy way to make sure your bullets line up is to start each one with a verb. Like this:

> When you use bullets, your customers will:
> - Read your copy quickly, because it's so easy to scan
> - Find all the info they want, at a glance
> - Focus on the most important parts of your message
> - Pay close attention to the copy before and after the bullets

As well as making sure your bullets all flow in one direction, this approach will give your copy a built-in sense of action. So suddenly the message feels more alive, more urgent.

Use punctuation wisely

When you're splitting a sentence, punctuation becomes a trusted ally. You've basically got 7 options:

Full stop
The humble full stop is top dog. It's telling the reader "That point has been made. Now let's move onto the next one."

In other words, you're locking in one piece of information. It's established now. So it's safe to proceed.

Comma
A well placed comma can have the same effect as a full stop, and it helps you to vary the pace. The sentence flows more easily, instead of stopping and starting.

Colon
A colon in the right place can be super powerful: it signals to the reader "here comes something important", because the next thing is usually the upshot of what's gone before.

Semi-colon
Bit of a dodgy one this. In formal writing, we're told to use them all the time; but for conversational copy, they're poison!

Reason: very few people know what a semi-colon is for. You might know that it's a break mid-sentence, but a good percentage of readers will just get confused. It's one to avoid.

Hyphen
Ah, the copywriter's best mate – the simple stroke that builds a nifty bridge between one part of a sentence and the next.

It's great for varying pace - so drop it in between two short sentences and you'll make one that's long but readable.

Plus, just like the colon, it has a natural sense of consequence - so the text that follows the hyphen often feels more important.

And used well, that's a great device for drawing attention – like this.

Ellipsis
Another copywriter's favourite, the series of three dots in a row...it's a great way to bridge two parts of a sentence.

It can work as an alternative to the colon or hyphen, implying consequence in the same way...but it's best used to give a sense of time passing, or suggesting there's more to say. Call it a substitute for "etc".

It's also popular in testimonials, to replace irrelevant words in between the juicy bits.

Example:

> "If I didn't have this product in the kitchen drawer, wrapped up in a small brown envelope, my life would be impossible"

Becomes:

> "If I didn't have this product...my life would be impossible"

Brackets
Brackets have their place (I admit, I use them) but at times they'll confuse the message - mainly because they're a home for embedded clauses.

OK, if you absolutely have to use an embedded clause (and I mean really have to) then yes, a bracket is a better device than a comma. To its credit, a bracket signals "here comes an embedded clause"...while a comma sneaks it in under the radar, just adding to the confusion!

Still, all things being equal, I'd keep brackets to a minimum – especially in actual sales copy, where an easy read can make all the difference.

Summing up
The uber sentence is one of your worst enemies. But you have a full arsenal to use against it, so deploy...and show no mercy!

The rule is: establish point one. Then move onto point two. Then onto point three. And so on. Don't say it all at once because you'll only confuse.

Remember what we said before about literacy standards...best make it easy!

AT A GLANCE

- ✓ Don't overload the sentence. Make one point at a time
- ✓ Break it down: what's the core info, and what are the consequences?
- ✓ Don't use embedded clauses, like this, because they're a distraction
- ✓ Keep the message tight by dropping redundant words
- ✓ Use synonyms to avoid repetition
- ✓ Vary the pace with bullets
- ✓ Make sure all your bullets flow in the same direction
- ✓ Use punctuation to steady the message and focus the eye on important words

*Vary the pace. But mostly,
keep your sentences short. Like this.*

– 5 –
Let it flow
Because making a point is more than throwing in random facts

So much copy feels disjointed. As you move from one paragraph to the next, it feels like the writer is making points at random – almost like saying "and another thing" instead of developing an argument.

When that happens, the copy loses momentum. Readers become less engaged. Most will wonder where the message is heading, and some will give up altogether.

And who can blame them? Life's too short.

So this chapter is all about flow. You've already got the know-how to write shorter, sharper sentences, and now we're going to join the dots to give the reader some kind of journey.

Here goes nothing:

Stay focused
The key to simple writing is linearity. One page or chapter or letter is about one thing and one thing only. If it's a spew of random bits and pieces, the reader gets confused.

Taking that further, one paragraph is also one thing only - just one small part of the big thing. So is the next one, and the next.

In other words, paragraphs should put your copy into neat little compartments, helping the reader through your message, one point at a time. So your job is to keep a tight focus in each paragraph...no drifting off into other topics that belong elsewhere.

Take this example, promoting a sale at an "everything for the home" store:

> Pop in this week for special offers on bedding, beds and bedroom furniture. Everything from duvets and pillow cases to single and double beds, wardrobes, dressers and bedside units. Plus a great deal on kitchens. Need a new hob? Come and see..

Woah! I thought we were talking bedrooms here, and suddenly we're down in the kitchen. What happened? I'm losing the thread.

Plus I've taken my eye off the bedroom deals just when it was getting exciting.

One paragraph, one purpose if you please! Then we all know where we stand.

Create relationships

If your paragraphs are disciplined, moving from point to point, the reader should get a sense of natural progression. And you can add to that by using segues – linking words that confirm the relationship between paragraph A and paragraph B.

Let's start with Paragraph A, because it's a very good place to start. Taking this example from an internal memo:

> [PARAGRAPH A]
> The customer management system will be offline for the next five days, while our IT contractors carry out essential upgrades. This is an unavoidable step caused by a series of programming errors.

Now let's look at a few different segues into Paragraph B:

The And Segue

Paragraph B builds on Paragraph A. It's expanding - acknowledging what's gone before and taking it forward. As in:

> [PARAGRAPH B]
> As well as removing bugs from the system, this project will give us a smart new way to stay in touch with our best customer groups.

Your linking words to open the paragraph will depend on context. But they might include:

- And
- Plus
- Also
- As well as
- More than
- Similarly
- In addition
- In fact
- Indeed
- Likewise
- Moreover
- Furthermore
- That includes
- Not to mention
- For example
- Not only that, but
- What's more
- You see,
- Above all
- Look at it this way

The But Segue

Paragraph B goes against Paragraph A. Maybe it offers another view that totally contradicts… but more likely, it just modifies the first statement.

As in:

> [PARAGRAPH B]
> However, you'll still be able to access customer records through a back-up database we've posted on the intranet.

Linking words to suit your context could include:

- But
- However
- Although
- Despite
- Even so
- Still
- Yet
- Mind you
- That said
- Then again
- Nonetheless
- On the other hand

The So Segue
This one's all about consequence. Paragraph B draws a conclusion based on Paragraph A. As in:

> [PARAGRAPH B]
> As a result, you'll have limited access to customer records this week.

Linking words in your context could be:

- So
- Therefore
- Consequently
- Then
- That's why
- That means
- That leads to
- As a result
- The upshot is
- By the end
- Down the line
- Voila!

The Emotive Segue
So far, our linking words have been purely functional. There's no emotion or value judgement – they just imply a factual link.

But there's one more type: the emotive segue that leads with your opinion.

This could work with an "and" statement:

> [PARAGRAPH B]
> Regrettably, this work will also affect the IT department. Any non-critical issues will have to wait until next week.

Or with a modifying "but" statement:

> [PARAGRAPH B]
> Fortunately though, the rest of our network will still be online.

Or it could work with a "so" statement:

> [PARAGRAPH B]
> Happily, this will improve our efficiency from next week onwards.

In your context, linking words might include:

- Regrettably
- Sadly
- Unfortunately
- Fortunately
- Happily
- Joyfully
- Significantly
- Interestingly
- Importantly
- Intriguingly
- Curiously
- Spookily

Just be aware – some linking words are not so conversational: words like "consequently", "therefore" and "furthermore" feel OTT. So ask yourself, is it a word your reader would use in conversation?

And just as importantly: does it feel right coming from you?

Use sub-headings
About 80-something percent of the time, you'll find that segues can create the link you want between paragraphs. But there are times when a simple linking word won't do it, because the copy has changed direction altogether.

When that happens, you need a sub-heading to flag the shift in focus. Like a sign at a fork in the road, a sub-head cuts through the confusion and tells the reader what lies ahead - so they can proceed with confidence.

Typically, a sub-heading should only be a few words. It could be one word only, or up to half a dozen. And of course, it should trail the copy that follows.

Here are some angles to try:

- Give a functional description
- Trail the emotional benefit
- Pick out a choice phrase or quotation

- Draw attention to something quirky
- Give an instruction
- Offer some advice
- Ask a question
- Lay down a challenge
- Give an ultimatum
- Make an offer

To some extent, the angle you choose will depend on what you're writing. For example, picking out a quotation is great for press releases. Advice works well in articles. An offer, challenge or ultimatum is best used in sales copy.

But don't be constrained by convention - just suck it and see what works for you.

There's more on headlines and different types of messages later on. For now, just bear in mind that sub-headings can come to the rescue when the reader starts to scream "Hang on, where are you going with this?"

Make it scanable
OK, I don't think "scanable" is a real word, but I guess you know what I mean: make the message easy to scan so the reader can see their way through the word maze.

This matters, because we all have our own way of reading things.

Some readers are impatient. They'll shy away from huge blocks of text, so they're drawn to the easy bits like headlines, sub-headings, pictures, captions and videos. If a quick scan shows them something of interest, they'll think about reading the whole thing.

Other people are more methodical and want to know every last detail. So grab their attention at the start and they'll read from left to right, top to bottom.

In practice, this means creating a "scanning path", so scanners can scan and readers read.

To make it scanable, you need a prominent headline plus a few choice sub-heads and a highly visible call to action at the foot of the page. Images should sit high up on the right hand side, and always include a caption. Incidental info, like statistics, should sit to the right, but lower down the page. All this leaves the main section clear for the body of the message.

Then there's one more tactic to consider...

After checking out images, the scanning reader will focus mostly on the left hand margin, and especially the sub-heads. That gives you another opportunity to catch his eye - by placing the most important words at the start of a new line.

Compare these two paragraphs:

> [VERSION A]
> I work with clients who want to be totally debt-free within 5 years. I review their financial commitments and the very latest interest rates, then find alternative deals.
>
> [VERSION B]
> You can get a better deal on finance. I'll help with a quick review to see if you can live debt-free within 5 years. All it takes is a short get-together, when you're ready.

Version B is more likely to grab attention, for two reasons:

First, it's about the customer and the end result - not the vendor and the process.

And second, look at the words that fall to the left hand side. It all sounds so much easier:

- Instead of a self-serving "I", there's "You"
- Instead of "debt", there's "help"
- Instead of heavy "financial commitments", there's "live debt-free"
- Instead of boring "interest rates", there's just "a short get-together"

If you were a scanner, which version would make you want to read more?

Summing up
When you start writing copy, flow is one of the major stumbling blocks. But it's incredibly easy to put it right, just by keeping paragraphs tight and confirming the link from one to the next. Make it scanable too, and readers will find their way through the message. Sorted.

Exactly how the message is structured, well that's another matter. We'll get to it later on.

For now, just get into the habit of easing the reader's journey from point to point.

AT A GLANCE

- ✓ Every page and paragraph has a single purpose
- ✓ Every paragraph links into the next
- ✓ Segues are functional or emotive statements, implying "and", "but" or "so"
- ✓ Use sub-headings to signal a major change in direction
- ✓ Create a scanning path for easy reading
- ✓ Images need captions to catch the wandering eye
- ✓ Use effortless words on the left side of the page

__Make life easy for the reader and he'll carry on reading. Confuse him, alienate him and you've lost him. Maybe forever.__

PART 2
WHO'S READING THIS ANYWAY?

"To understand the man, you must first walk a mile in his moccasin."

North American Indian Proverb

– 6 –
Your language - or theirs?
*A bit of mirroring now,
just for good measure*

Earlier on, I mentioned my previous life pounding the streets of South Wales, selling cable TV.

One week I'd be out in a leafy suburb, talking politely to solicitors, bank managers and other professional types. The next I'd be on a council estate, lapsing into my best Valleys accent and rarely minding my Ps and Qs...basically mirroring every customer.

Now if I'd just been natural me out there, I guess I'd have done OK – especially in the leafier spots, because I'm ever so nice and quietly spoken by nature! But I wouldn't have sold as much as I did, because I'd have lacked the extra connection.

Every decent sales person knows this inside out. Many will morph from door to door, becoming a subtle reflection of the person they're talking to.

And yet, ask a typical sales rep to put something in writing, and they'll throw that knowledge out of the window. Some will revert to the pseudo-professional style we've already looked at, while others will stick to their own voice – forgetting their customers altogether.

And sometimes you have to bend your voice towards the other guy.

Up 'til now, we've been working to bring out *your* natural voice, and write clear, simple copy that reflects the way *you* talk. But now it's time to spare a thought for the customer too...what influence should he have on your wording and style?

Quick answer: every case will be different. Sometimes it's a few small changes, other times it's a total overhaul.

To take an extreme, let's say you're a 50-something exec selling mobile apps to teenagers. Frankly, even your "at home" voice is going to be out of place - and you can't compensate with a load of "LOL" and "ROFL", because that'll just be embarrassing.

At best, you'll sound like a part-time dad trying to bond with his kids by rapping.

So in that event, you'd need to find a writer who's closer to the audience. Someone who can write in a way that's real and "down with the kids"!

But in most markets, the difference between your language and theirs will be less dramatic. Generally, you can still be the natural you, and just make a few small changes like adapting tone or dropping in the odd familiar phrase.

The end result might not be 100% the way you talk. But if it means something to the customer…and it doesn't look out of place…then hey, that's business innit?

So how do you get to know your customer's style of language?

Well, first off you have to know who your customer is…and that's a challenge in its own right!

Most people just use a broad category to define their target market, like "business owners" or "senior citizens" or even just "consumers". Some have tighter niches, so they can say "restaurant owners" or "dog lovers" or whatever…but even then, the prospect himself is a riddle wrapped in an enigma.

"Well we know he likes dogs…but what else?"

"Dunno!"

"What's he like as a person?"

"Dunno!"

You see the predicament?

There's an easy way around this, though – just think of it like this:

You've already met your ideal customer... somewhere, at some time in your life.

Another story: I owe a huge debt to a man called Phil. He's not a nice man – he's bad tempered, impatient, downright rude at times. But he's also one smart cookie. And many moons back, for a few unpleasant months, he was my boss.

Phil didn't suffer fools. And when he summoned you into his office, he made that crystal clear. If you wanted to keep your job, you quickly learned to cut the waffle and jargon. You just gave him the facts. Hard and fast, no sugar coating.

I still remember the fledgling exec who gave him a presentation – and took the insane career step of including bits of clip art. From the other end of the corridor, I could hear Phil roar, "I don't pay you to **** about with pretty pictures. What have you sold???"

The poor exec came out battered and bruised, and probably wanting his mum. But hopefully with a lesson learned: talk to Phil in Phil's language, or suffer his wrath.

Thankfully, I ditched the corporate world quite a few years ago. But I still think of Phil every day. Because when I'm writing anything that targets a senior manager, in my own mind I'm writing to him.

No-one else.

Just Phil.

I know that if the copy is tight enough to get past his filters – if it's free of "dressing" and unproven claims and other irritations – then it stands every chance of striking a chord with other MDs and CEOs.

True, each individual reader won't be Phil to a tee. But as senior managers, they'll share enough of his traits - and most will respond to the same type of down-to-earth, no-frills, no B.S. copy.

OK...so where does that leave you?

You might not know your prospects (or even your customers) in person. But if you search through the thousands of people you've met over the years, you've definitely known someone who fits the mould of your average buyer.

Someone who shares your customers' interests ...someone with the same temperament...the same fears, the same ambitions, the same way of talking...

You will know someone!

And it doesn't matter if they're dead or alive, or living on the other side of the world – because you don't have to bring them back into your life. Just assume you're writing - or talking - to them.

I use this approach all the time. If my prospect is technically-minded, I'm addressing a geeky IT Whizz I worked with in my first job.

If they're early retired or planning for old age, fine - I've got aunts and uncles.

See what I mean?

So, let's get going by flicking through your mind's own little black book...

You might as well start with your customer list and ask the obvious question: who is Mr Typical – the archetype who sums up your whole customer base (or at least a sizeable chunk)?

If you draw a blank there, think of prospects who you know well enough to talk to. Or other business contacts. Staff, suppliers, associates and so on.

Or look into other parts of your life – Your Phil is out there somewhere!

If you sell mainly to consumers, you could start by roaming through Facebook. Call up a list of your friends and ask yourself who makes the grade.

In the same way, if you sell B2b, take a look at your LinkedIn contacts. Go through the same process.

Now if you're still without a match, dig deeper.

Think about all the people you've met at every stage of your life. Friends and family, work colleagues, bosses, teachers, neighbours and so on.

Or think about the real people you see on TV.

Or failing that, the characters in your favourite shows, or books or films. That's a last resort, because they're not real people...but do it if you have to!

I'll say with confidence, by now you should have someone in mind...

Now – think how you'd speak to him.

At this stage, we're just looking to apply some instinct to the conversation. Later on, we'll come back to Your Phil and see how he can help us to map out the whole message...but for now, while we're developing the basic tone of voice, let's focus on his way of talking – and how you can adopt it.

Now don't fret over this, because I'll promise you it's a skill you've already mastered. In the real world, we all mirror others without even knowing it. You'll use one voice for your Great Auntie Maud, another for your boss, another for your bessie mate, etc. And you'll do it all instinctively.

You don't have to over-think this.

That said, maybe your mind is more analytical than spontaneous. So if you'd rather approach the task academically, try recalling a conversation and noting how Your Phil comes across.

You'll want to think of the words he uses, as well as other clues like body language and tone of voice. Then ask yourself a few questions:

- What type of words and phrases will he find acceptable?
- What type of words – if any – are likely to confuse him?
- What words will he find corny, offensive or insincere?
- Does he overuse – or even misuse - certain words?
- What references will he understand?
- Is he verbose or to the point?
- Warm or aggressive?
- Blunt or diplomatic?
- Patient or impatient?
- Approachable or distant?
- Open-minded or blinkered?

You can probably add to the list as you make your observations. But don't get bogged down in analysis.

You just want to *find a level* where you can talk to him and hold his attention.

Putting it into practice
Once you're confident that you've got the measure of Your Phil, go back to your Practice Message and adapt it, just for him. Don't

abandon your own voice - that's a big no! Just lean towards him a little.

When you've done that, I'm guessing it will sound like a simple conversation. It should feel informal or semi-formal, with a good mix of your style and his.

Not only that, you should notice that things from Part One fall into place. You're talking in straight simple sentences, using everyday words and it's all flowing neatly from one point to the next.

Well at least, that's the idea!

But if it still feels more like a letter to the bank manager, all is not lost. You could always try making some real life observations.

The easiest way is to have a real chat with Your Phil himself. (Don't contact him yet though...there's more on "probing" Phil in chapter 7, so read ahead before you pick up the phone).

Alternatively, if chatting to Your Phil is out of the question, try talking to some customers instead.

Failing that, see how your customers interact with you online. See what they post on your

Facebook page, how they reply to your tweets or emails, how they comment on your blog posts...even how they troll you in forums!

A spot of cyber-snooping could go a long way here. Where else can you find them discussing issues relating to you and your market? Check LinkedIn groups and consumer blogs, or search for trending topics on twitter.

Offline, there's a load of material too. Take a look at the testimonials your clients have written for you. Or talk to people at trade shows and business networks, or wherever your paths might cross.

It's all out there waiting for you, in one guise or another.

Once you've gathered up a sample of comments, do some quick analysis. Get a feel for common words and phrases and patterns in their speech. Again, you don't have to formally measure this stuff – but if that's your thing, just go back and review the list of questions above.

It won't be long before you see a strong pattern emerging, and a style of language that you can use to show you're "one of the gang"!

Summing up
You already know the customer through your own experience - so you can talk the way he talks and second guess the way he's thinking. It's the first step in writing to him in a natural, conversational style.

If you're selling to more than one type of customer, no problem – just do it again. However broad your market is, you can narrow your customers down to a finite number of types (say half a dozen or so).

Each type will have his own way of talking, so run through this "getting to know you" phase and see how your copy changes.

Is it starting to feel like a conversation?

AT A GLANCE

- ✓ Search your mind for the ideal customer
- ✓ Focus on who he is…not what he does
- ✓ Explore his way of talking
- ✓ Adapt your message to suit his personal style
- ✓ Make sure it's mainly you, but with a touch of him
- ✓ Do this for every customer segment

***From now on, walk the tightrope…
between his natural voice and yours***

– 7 –
What's eating Phil?
*Finding buttons to push,
before you start pushing*

By now you've practiced the knack of writing in your natural voice, with a nod towards the customer's style of language. The rest of Part Two is all about making a stronger connection: knowing the customer, then grabbing attention and keeping it relevant.

So let's get going by getting to know Your Phil a little better.

Phil's Insomnia Button
Something...I don't know what...is keeping Your Phil awake at night.

He could be wrestling with a problem or savouring an opportunity. But either way it's something that really matters to him, deep down.

We'll call this his Insomnia Button - and you have to understand it so you can push it later on.

So...what is it? And why does it matter?

Well, "what is it?" is easy enough, because it's probably linked to the widget or service you're selling. Maybe he's thinking of buying a laptop, or converting the attic, or going to see the pyramids. Or pretty much anything, really.

But "why does it matter?"...that's something else. There could be any number of reasons. But don't despair, there is one thing you can be certain of:

He doesn't want the thing itself - he wants the impact of having that thing.

Take the laptop example. Trust me, he has no wish to own a lump of plastic, metal and wires. But he does want the convenience of working anywhere, any time. Or the efficiency that gives him. Or the entertainment he can access. Or just the sheer kudos of being the guy with the latest model.

Converting the attic: he doesn't want another room, he wants breathing space. Maybe a quiet escape, or a chance to pursue an interest, or a cure for living in an overcrowded house.

Seeing the Pyramids: he wants a great experience, a memory, or a chance to brag about it.

Never the thing itself...just the impact of having the thing.

You can relate this to any purchase. A drill buys you a better home...a sofa buys you comfort...a squash racquet buys you fun, or a longer life...

We don't do anything unless there's some emotion egging us on.

If it helps, you can relate the emotion to some basic impulse. It could be freedom, self-worth, gratification, comfort, security, hope, health, prosperity, convenience, survival, belonging...or any other primitive urge that leads to a safer, better, easier life.

But if you'd rather keep things simple, look at it this way instead: it's all about gaining pleasure, or avoiding pain.

It's true. You pay your rent or mortgage to avoid the misery of living in a high rise block or sleeping in a box. If you live in a swanky pad, you've upgraded from the basic hut for the added pleasure it brings.

Go to Tesco and buy a tin of Lo-cost Beans 'n' Sausage, and you're avoiding the misery of starving to death. Go to M&S and buy their Finest Oak Smoked Pheasant In Sun-Dried

Tomato & Basil Puree, then I guess there's some added pleasure. If you like that sort of thing.

Some purchases, like holidays, are only driven by pleasure. Others, like insurance, are purely driven by pain. And others, like cars, have a mix of the two - the pleasure of comfort, status and freedom, while avoiding the pain of doing without, or coping with an old banger.

Even "selfless" deeds like charity fall into the same bucket. Not to deride anyone who gives to a noble cause, but it's either for the good feeling of helping your fellow man or to avoid the pain of watching another human being suffer.

So - when it comes to Your Phil and his Insomnia Button, it pays to think beyond the widget: what's the pleasure or pain involved?

It's worth spending a while chewing over this, because once you know the pressure point you've got untold ammunition.

If you're writing a blog or article, you'll know what advice and information he wants. And if you're writing a sales page, you know what he'll be asking before he says yes.

So...push button when ready

OK, let's say you know what he wants and why he wants it. That feels like a good time for a trial push of the button.

So think back to your Practice Message and the adaptations you've made. What changes should you make now, so you lead with the pleasure or pain?

Here's a quick example of how a message might look, before and after.

> [BEFORE - WITHOUT PLEASURE OR PAIN]
> I'm a personal trainer, and I offer a wide range of services including diet control and personal exercise plans to keep my clients in peak condition. I tailor plans for every client because different bodies have different stress points and respond to different stimuli. Diet control is also important, because it's essential to have the right mix of nutrients and protein in order to maximise physical activity.
>
> [AND AFTER - WITH PLEASURE OR PAIN]
> Look, you already know the importance of diet and exercise. You know how great you feel after a healthy meal or a workout, and how rubbish you feel after eating fast food or vegging out on the sofa. On paper, you know all that - but committing to a healthy lifestyle is a different matter, isn't it? I get

it, you've got temptations and distractions everywhere you go. So my job, as a personal trainer, is to keep you focused on getting into shape - and staying there.

The first version is focused on the trainer and his processes, and as a result it feels quite distant and a bit preachy. But the second version turns it around. It leads with a mix of pleasure and pain, and shows some empathy for the customer. It's also more conversational - so all in, the message should hit home.

Now...over to you.

We're going to hold a trial "conversation" with Your Phil. We'll pitch him an idea, and see how he responds.

Woah! Hang on, we're gonna do what now? Pitch him an idea??

Yep. Stay with me, it's just a mental exercise - an extension of the language exercise we did in Chapter 6. Only this time we're moving from words and style, and onto the message itself.

I know this might feel odd at first, like some drama school improv exercise. But you don't have to wear a leotard or pretend to be a tree...and it's all going on inside your mind, where no-one else is watching!

We've all rehearsed important conversations in the past, and this is nothing different.

OK? Time to find a quiet space and get lost inside your own head:

Let's assume you're meeting Your Phil for the first time, maybe at some networking bash or other such gathering. You've gone through the niceties, and he's told you about all about him...now it's your turn to jump in – starting with some pleasure or pain, and ending with the promise of changing his life for the better.

Think hard. Imagine his face and body language as you run through your spiel. Which bits make him wince? Where does he look bored? When do you see the lightbulb moment, where your message clicks into place? And what does he ask you before he shows a definite interest?

You might want to play this out in your head a few times over, because the answers to those questions will be the backbone of your message. Every time (in your head!) that he cringes or looks puzzled, annoyed or frustrated, he's showing you the hurdles. He doesn't believe you, or it doesn't make sense, or he can't see what's in it for him. Or he's sceptical, or he's somehow got the wrong end of the stick.

Basically, he's telling you what does and doesn't work in your pitch – so you'll know how to adapt any kind of message from here on in.

Now before we go any further...does this exercise work for you?

It might not. As noted in the language exercise, some minds are too analytical for this kind of fantasy thinking. If that's you, then as noted last time, you'll be better off making it real. Try talking to your Phil in person. Or failing that, hit the business networks, or trade shows, or stake out any place where Your Phil is likely to be.

Hold a real conversation...then go back through the analysis.

Next: jot down your pitch and observations
Once you've had the real or virtual chat, you've probably gauged Your Phil's response. So a useful next step is to write up the pitch, and highlight the significant points: the places that seem to work, and those that need a re-think.

You should be able to mark up the most effective phrases, plus the benefits that hit home and the moments that invite objections.

Then adapt it, so you've got something more workable next time.

Now, if you're writing sales copy, you've got a basic structure right there - something that marketing legend Dan Kennedy calls *Problem, Agitate, Resolve*. You could use that to good effect...but we'll look at structure in much more detail when we get to Part Three, just to give you a few more options.

Alternatively, if you're writing a lead gen or factual piece, this exercise should just give you an instinctive feel for where your message is heading. You know what holds his attention now, and what pushes his buttons....but your message still needs structure. Again, more in Part Three.

Summing up
There's no such thing as a non-emotive purchase. Even the smallest, most functional thing, like a bag of nails, has some emotion in there somewhere. It might not be obvious at first glance, but if you keep on asking what the nails are for and why, you'll find an emotion at the end.

Like seeing the smile on the face of the person in the picture that you're hanging on the wall!

To find Your Phil's Insomnia Button and turn it into a workable pitch, you might well be stepping outside your comfort zone. But it's worth persevering, because there's no substitute for latching onto your prospect's real emotional hooks. Whether you do it in person or tucked away in your imagination, it's giving you a starting point that's based on some genuine human behaviour.

So give it a whirl...it will pay off in spades when you come to the actual writing.

AT A GLANCE

- ✓ Find the *Insomnia Button* that keeps Your Phil awake at night
- ✓ He doesn't want the thing - he wants the impact of having the thing
- ✓ Will your solution add some pleasure or remove some pain?
- ✓ Adapt your Practice Message, leading with pleasure or pain
- ✓ Finish by showing how his life can change for the better
- ✓ Pitch it: virtually or for real, whatever works best
- ✓ Note response and adapt the message 'til it works

Every penny or dime we spend is driven by an emotional impulse. Identify it, serve it and business will always follow.

– 8 –
Starting the conversation
Writing headlines that grab attention...
WITHOUT SCREAMING AT THE READER!!!

Every message starts with a headline. Whether it's factual copy, lead generation or a sales piece, you have to grab the reader's attention if you want them to read on.

And (with just a few exceptions) the best copy has always done the deed with the big fat words right up there at the top of the page.

So in this chapter, we're going to look at different types of headline - while remembering our mission: keep it conversational.

Quick aside: for most of this book, I've talked about conversational copy mostly as the antidote to corporate waffle. But now we get to headlines, we should spare a thought for the second evil of the copywriting world:

Overblown bullish hype.

Headlines, especially online, are easy prey for merchants of hype. I don't know about you, but I retch every time I see something like this:

••

REVEALED! The ultimate butt-kicking miracle <u>cash-spewing</u> **instant wealth machine** that's got THE WORLD'S SMARTEST BILLIONAIRES crawling over broken glass and literally BEGGING ON THEIR KNEES FOR A TINY SLICE OF THE ACTION
<u>GUARANTEE:</u> spend 20 minutes a month on this and <u>IN 48 HOURS</u> you can CHOOSE YOUR FIRST LUXURY YACHT, with a crew of NAKED NYMPHOMANIAC SUPER MODELS.
<u>Yours TODAY for $12</u>

••

Tacky in-yer-face headlines like this are mostly found flogging get-rich-quick tat, marital aids and dodgy fitness products. But more and more, they're cropping up in the mainstream too. If you've ever had a letter from a will writer, you'll know exactly what I mean:

!!!WARNING!!!
If you DIE WITHOUT LEAVING A WILL,
the government will SEIZE YOUR HOUSE,
kidnap your wife and EAT YOUR CHILDREN.
Is that what you want? Well, is it??

Well, slight exaggeration maybe. But the point is, no industry is safe from this evil breed of aggressive hype-driven headlines.

So, how can you grab the reader's attention without resorting to BS or angry scare tactics?

Easy really. Just appeal to his ever-selfish nature.

Headline Type #1: Pure Self Interest

By now, you've spent some time getting to know Your Phil's Insomnia Button. So appealing to his selfish side should be a breeze. Just promise to solve his biggest issue, and you can expect him to read on.

Example: let's say you're a bank, offering a great deal on loans. And the Insomnia Button is "how to cope with a growing mountain of debts". In that case, a simple self-interest headline would be:

> Get rid of all your debts and make one easy payment a month

So far so good. It certainly speaks to Phil's self interest. But still, it could make better use of his emotional state. "Get rid of all your debts" is functional and doesn't really touch on the angst of coping with mounting debts. Then "make one easy payment a month" feels like a burden. Even if it's better than his current situation, it still smacks of effort.

So as an alternative, how about this:

> No more crippling repayments...just one easy deposit a month

Looking better now. The first half ("crippling repayments") focuses on the pain of debt, and the second half feels effortless, because we've lost the action of making the payment. Note how the word "make" has been left out, while "easy payment" is now "easy deposit".

We're getting there. But still, I'm sure Phil has seen this kind of promise time and again - so I doubt we've gone far enough to convince him this is different (and therefore worthy of his attention).

No problem. You've done your homework on Phil, so you already know his objections. And that means you can ask yourself, what's holding him back?

- Is it apathy? *"Hey, it's no big deal, it can wait 'til another day..."*
- Or laziness? *"Yeah, sounds OK, but is it worth the effort...?"*
- Or scepticism? *"I dunno, it sounds too good to be true..."*
- Or a misconception? *"They don't mean me, I wouldn't qualify..."*

One easy way to address these objections is to add a sub-heading, just below the main headline. So remember, we start with:

No more crippling repayments...just one easy deposit a month

Then if we're tackling apathy, the sub-heading might say:

Secure a limited fixed term deal, for October only

Or to tackle laziness, we might say:

Switching is easy: make a simple 2-minute call and it's done

To tackle scepticism, how about:

Secure our lowest interest rate since 2007

Finally, to tackle the misconception, try:

Exclusive offer for long-standing customers only

Of course, you might be dealing with all those objections together - so maybe you need a longer sub-heading. Something along these lines:

An exclusive offer for our long-standing customers, this October:
Make a 2-minute call to secure our lowest interest rate since 2007

This way, whatever Phil's objection, he should agree to read on. He's got a reason to believe you, and a reason to go ahead.

Quick aside: in this example, we've addressed objections in the sub-heading. But there are other ways too. You could also:

- Expand the headline, so it grabs attention *and* fights the objection
- Use a "call-out" to let the reader know you're talking to them: either with a line of text above or below the headline, or a design feature like text in a box or circle
- Use design features or bullet points to trail the main benefits

---

Headline Type #2: Curiosity

The job of the headline is to get the reader into the first paragraph. Then the first paragraph is there to make sure he reads the second. And so on.

And sometimes, you can draw him in with a dash of curiosity.

Of course, ultimately we're still appealing to his selfish nature. But this is a different way of telling him how he's going to benefit. Because while the *Pure Self Interest* headline tells the entire story, a *Curiosity* headline has to hold something back.

So taking our bank loans example, you could use curiosity like this:

> How many hours do you have to work every month to pay off your debts?

Or:

> The easy way to stop your debts from spiraling out of control

In both versions, you can see the mix of self-interest and curiosity: both refer to a problem, and tease the reader with a hint of a solution.

Let's take another example.

You're a fitness trainer and you've found some research saying one in five children will be obese by the age of 10. The research stresses the impact on a child's health and social development, and you're using all this as a trigger to promote a junior bootcamp.

Your message is going out to parents of 8-9 year olds. So how should you start?

Compare these options:

[VERSION A]
One in every five children will be obese by the age of 10

Versus:

[VERSION B]
An urgent health warning for one in every five children

Versus:

[VERSION C]
Why doctors say one in five children will face a rough ride in high school

Now let's see how they match up:

Version A
Curiosity Value: zero. The headline gives you the whole story, so why bother reading on?

Self Interest: low. It's there, but it's limited because we can't see the consequence.

Therefore: the headline might grab attention, but it's not likely to lure the reader deeper into the story.

Version B
Curiosity Value: good. It holds some info back, so the reader wants answers.

Self Interest: good. Not many parents would ignore an "urgent health warning" for children.

Therefore: parents will probably read past the headline - at least until they find out what the warning means.

Version C
Curiosity Value: high. It's more than a self-contained statement, it leads into the content below. Why will kids face a rough ride? And what's the link between doctors and high school?

Self Interest: high. Every good parent wants to spare their child from trauma. And the fact that doctors are worried makes it feel real and urgent.

Therefore: parents are likely to carry on past the headline, to see how their children are affected.

I should stress, I haven't formally tested these headlines against each other. I've only run a small and unscientific sample.

However, my beer mat findings have certainly backed the assertion: C is strongest by far, because it scores the highest on both counts.

Headline Type #3: Revelations

Similar to curiosity, you can hook the reader by telling him something new and important. In B2b, that's probably a new development within his industry, or a wider issue that affects businesses all over. In B2c, it could be an incident or trend that's going to impact on his home life, family or outside interests.

Key to writing this one is *how* you break the news. Let's say you're a Health & Safety Consultant writing to small business owners in response to new legislation.

Compare these options:

[VERSION A]
DID YOU KNOW?
The new *Safety At Work Act* allows your employees to sue for 5 years salary if they injure themselves on the job!!

Versus:

[VERSION B]
No business can afford to be sued for 5 years salary. So let's make sure you're ready for the new *Safety At Work Act*...

Version A gives the information, but in a brash way that says "Look at me, I'm clever because I knew this before you!".

Tacky tricks like challenging the reader's knowledge and ending with an exclamation mark make the whole message feel underhand, sensationalist and predatory - which is not at all appropriate for the audience and circumstances.

Upshot: the reader might be horrified by the revelation - but he probably won't want to do business with the smug little slime ball behind it.

Version B is less aggressive. Instead of being the happy bearer of bad news, the writer is simply saying "How can I help you deal with this?"

Think about that...who would you rather deal with?

The interesting thing here is that Version B assumes the reader has already heard the news - therefore showing some respect for the reader's intelligence.

And that changes the way the message is received.

If the reader has heard about it, he won't get defensive and mutter "So what else is new?"...more likely, he'll read on because he knows he has a problem.

On the other hand, if he hasn't heard the news, he'll read on to find out more. And he'll feel he can trust the writer because of the friendly, respectful tone.

Finding inspiration
So far, all this is great in theory. But when you're staring at a blank page, is it really going to help?

Maybe not. So below I've listed 30 headline triggers. Try using these as inspiration, just to get some ideas flowing.

My advice is write down every idea that comes to you - good or bad - until you've got half a dozen headlines that feel right or thereabouts. Then you can check for the essentials - self-interest, curiosity and revelation - to adapt and whittle down the contenders 'til you have a winner.

Just one word of advice: if you think of something awesome at the top of the list, keep going...there could be something even better further down.

Headline triggers:
to start the conversation

1. Start telling a story
2. Ask a question
3. Give a command or instruction
4. Make a promise
5. Offer advice
6. Make a recommendation
7. Make a comparison
8. Give an expert warning
9. Lay down a challenge
10. Share a secret
11. Give some good news
12. Give an ultimatum
13. Use a testimonial
14. Speak to his natural scepticism
15. Highlight the price or offer
16. Stress your guarantee
17. Offer something exclusive
18. Describe the end result
19. Link to current events
20. Ask if he needs your product

21. Offer to save him money
22. Offer to save him time
23. Tell him what he'll never have to do again
24. Tell him how to avoid a common mistake
25. Compare your widget with the norm
26. Tease him with a hint of the solution
27. Tantalise – put the benefit within his grasp
28. Describe a bizarre use for the widget
29. Describe what the widget isn't, or what it won't do
30. Promise the benefit, without the usual drawback

Most "triggers" can be used for all three types of headline. Inevitably though, some will suit one type more than others. For example, telling a story is great for curiosity, a comparison suits self interest and an expert warning suits revelation. Try it and see what works for you.

Final thought: some headlines we've looked at here focus on the pain. Some focus on the solution. Others focus on one, then the other. You should trial this to see which option works best for you.

As a rule, I'd avoid headlines that focus solely on the pain, and favour one of these options:

- Positive headlines, followed by pain (or aspiration) in the main message
- Headlines that couple the pain with the solution
- Headlines that lead with pain and suggest the solution will follow

Summing up
The message is all about the reader - and it all starts with the headline. When you promise to address his burning issue, he'll sit up and take notice.

You can do it by appealing directly to his sense of self interest, or push the selfish button through curiosity or revelation.

Just beware: if you use curiosity or revelation without a hint of self interest, he might get past the headline but he'll desert you soon after - unless the message quickly switches to his selfish agenda.

AT A GLANCE

- ✓ Experiment with different types of headline: self interest, curiosity or revelation
- ✓ For pure self interest headlines, try handling a common objection up front
- ✓ For curiosity headlines, remember to hold some info back
- ✓ For revelations, break the news with a friendly, supportive tone
- ✓ Revelations and curiosity fade quickly without self interest
- ✓ Use call-outs, sub-headings or other prominent text to confirm who you're talking to
- ✓ Test focusing on the solution against focusing on the pain

A headline starts the conversation on the reader's terms. It won't make the sale on its own...but it will start the ball rolling.

– 9 –
The You Factor
For every reader asking "What's In It For Me?"

Last time, we looked at headlines. And it was all about Your Phil - never about you.

Now if you're a frequent advertiser in your local rag, I know that goes against everything your ad rep has ever told you. I know you've been told to use your business or product name as a headline, then talk about yourself in the text below - usually next to a picture of "the team", all smiling with their thumbs up. But the sad truth is, that kind of self-centred copy never, ever works.

Because in reality, no-one cares about your business. Not one tiny jot.

They don't care about your mission statement or your processes or your brand, or your certificates that show a deep commitment to excellence in everything you do. It might be hard to accept, but it's true.

They don't give a flying hootenanny.

But it's not all bad news, because they do care what your business can do for them. It's a subtle but major difference that should have a massive impact on the way you write.

It means you don't harp on about yourself, singing your own praises. Instead, you write about the customer...Your Phil...and what matters to him.

So this chapter is all about building on the headline - staying focused on the customer from start to finish.

With the help of a few nifty tricks...

Add an invisible "so what?"
Whatever you say, the reader will always be asking the same old question: so what?

If you tell them about your background or business credentials, so what? They'll only care if you explain how that helps you to help them. And if you tell them what your product or service does, so what? They don't want to know about features, they want to see the benefits.

This is one of the fundamentals in the copywriting rulebook. A feature, if you don't know, is what your product does, while a benefit is what it does to improve things for the user. And a feature is irrelevant unless there's a benefit behind it.

Example: say you're selling a digital camera, with a built-in editing suite. Well that's a great feature - but it's not a benefit. The benefit is the chance to make the best of every photo you take.

Now that's a step in the right direction. But still, as benefit statements go, "make the best of every photo" is a bit bland and generic. So if you can, think about your audience and what the benefit means to them.

Let's say you're mailing to a list of affluent people aged over 60. OK, now you can talk about how they'll use the camera and the editing suite.

You could talk about the thrills of travelling the world, taking in the sights from the deck of a luxury cruise ship. They only get one chance to snap their favourite landmarks, and the editing suite will make sure every pic is the best it can be.

Or tell a story of the proud grandmother, grabbing a shot of her grandson crossing the line on school sports day – and removing the glare of the sun that spoilt the original pic.

You see how it works. The closer you get to the audience, the more the benefits hit home.

For some reason though, this basic step is still ignored by many. Even professional copywriters will sometimes let it slide and just focus on generic benefits, or even stick to features – while the reader yells "What's in it for me?"

Get to the point early
Just recently, I had a 24-page sales letter posted through my front door, put together in the form of a glossy brochure. On the front page, a lonely headline read:

> Ladies. I am going to make you so proud.

Not the best headline, for all the reasons we've already covered. But being a junk mail junkie, I waded through nonetheless.

Reading on, the copy talked endlessly about the importance of good housekeeping, then finally switched to the art and science of cleaning glass. At first, I wondered if it was selling a "miracle product" or business opportunity, but 10 pages later it all became clear: it was...

A window cleaning service!!

For now, let's sidestep the hot political spud of assuming women do all the housework! The letter sucked because it led with an obscure benefit (pride) and didn't offer a tangible context until we were 10 pages in.

All that time, I was yelling out "How will you make us proud???"

See, you can make me (or Mrs D) proud in umpteen billion ways. Log onto Amazon and post a nice review of this book. Or come round our house and help our son pass his GCSEs!

So yes, tell us *how* you'll make us proud and you might have our attention. But trust me, the Daniels ain't sitting at home day after day just waiting for someone – anyone – to give us back our pride by any old means.

Remember, I gave this letter the time of day because I'm a sad obsessive when it comes to this sort of thing. As a rule, others won't be willing to wade in without good reason. So while I don't know what kind of business it pulled in, I doubt that it covered the cost of printing. Simply because it failed to get to the point.

Big lesson: customers who don't know you from Adam won't take the time to go on a mystery trip.

Use the reader's frame of reference

Another story: some guy walked up to me quite recently at a business event and launched straight into his standard pitch. I can't recall it word for word, because my brain started to melt half way through it. But I can tell you it went something like this:

> "I'm a Supplier Cost Management Consultant, working with supply chains to maximise efficiencies and examine cost saving capabilities. Through two-way collaboration, I bring about minimised overheads and reduce the billing impact client-side. Invariably, the cross-party gains will mitigate the initial outlay and place the supplier relationship on a solid footing for long-term mutual growth."

Yep, it was one of those elevator pitches that needed 50 floors.

Like everyone else he'd spoken to that night, I wanted to run a mile. But instead, I quizzed him a little, then told him (nicely) that perhaps he could have said something like this:

> "Have you ever checked an invoice and wondered why it's so high? Well maybe it's because your supplier has got huge overheads to cover, or just hasn't found the most efficient way of working.

> But if I worked with them, I could help to bring their costs down and agree a better deal for you. So everybody wins."

He smirked and walked away, then bombarded someone else with his original pitch.

OK, I guess you can't help some people. I dare say he's still out there today, and still cocking it up big style.

Aside from the corporate guff he was spouting, the real sin was his frame of reference. By talking about his work in theoretical terms, I didn't relate to it one little bit. And neither did anyone else in the room, judging by the number of people avoiding him by the end of the night.

But if he'd gone with the suggestion above, he could have made a connection. He could have latched onto a problem that everyone in business has had at some time. It would all have fallen into place.

Heck, someone might have even taken his business card!

The big lesson when you're writing copy is, refer to the reader's own experience. How can you relate your message to their world, so it all seems real, relevant and practical – instead of some abstract thing that only matters to other people?

Get Specific

A few years ago, a car drove into the back of me on a roundabout. Result: minor whiplash and a barrage of "no win, no fee" solicitations.

One solicitor's letter stood out:

> Dear Mr Daniel
> I understand you have been involved in a road traffic accident which wasn't your fault. [COMPANY NAME] can help. We deal with legal claims including land registry, disputes between neighbours, personal injury and employment contracts. Our service is second to none blah blah blah.... and so on.

He then went on to tell me a bit about personal injury, and included a testimonial from a business owner who'd worked with him on a HR matter! Mmm...

A tad mind-boggling, methinks. This guy knew 100% that I'd been involved in an accident, and yet he chose to play the field and offer me every one of his services! I'm sure he reasoned "Hey, Mr D might be having a fight with next door, or running a business with a tricky employee, and if you don't ask, you don't get!"...but in practice, it made him look desperate and inefficient.

Plus, he missed the chance to address the real issue in detail.

If you're a fan of "The Simpsons" (who isn't?), this wasn't a million miles from Lionel Hutz, the iffy attorney who does shoe repairs on the side!

The take-away: make a clearly defined offer to a clearly defined audience, and you'll sell more widgets than the man with the megaphone standing on the street corner shouting "Come and have a look at our wares!"

Now maybe that's obvious, but still it's a rule that gets violated every day. So when you're writing copy, the message is ALWAYS BE SPECIFIC.

In practice, that means giving every message one clear purpose. Instead of trying to be all things to all people, focus the reader on one specific product, service or offer at a time.

It also means getting highly specific with the details. Numbers, dates, deadlines, benefits etc. will always mean more to the reader if they're definite, not abstract.

Tip the You balance
Once you've followed these principles, you should find that your copy says "You" and "Your" more than "I", "We", "Us" and "Our". In fact, it's almost impossible to apply this stuff and still be more "We"!

A quick sanity check won't hurt though. So try counting and comparing – or search online for something like "customer focus calculator" or "we we monitor". It'll do the job for you.

Now don't get me wrong here. "We" and "Our" et al still have a part to play in your message. But they should be there as a cameo, with "You" and "Your" in the starring role.

Even "We" can be "You" in disguise
In a sales message, it's easy to stay focused on the customer. But what about times when you're expected to talk about yourself?

There's your LinkedIn profile, "About Us" page, "Meet The Team"...or the sidebars and boxes that say "Who am I?" in other materials. People go there because they want to know something about you - don't they?

Well kind of. They want to know who you are, to be sure you're the best choice. But remember what we said earlier - The Invisible "So What?":

They don't want to know about you...they want to know how you can help them.

So instead of narrating your CV, try relating your background to their needs. Tell the story of why you do what you do...how your experiences have shaped the product or service you offer.

An example would be the restaurant owner who set up to offer a very particular kind of dining experience: it's the evening out he always wanted, but he couldn't find it anywhere else. And now he's able to offer you xyz...

From his story, we can pick up something about him and his values. But ultimately we're still focusing on what he can do for us.

And that's a million miles from insisting he's the best or droning on about his people and commitment to customer service.

This nifty little approach can work in pretty much any business, and adds a human face to even the sternest corporate brand.

Just start out talking "we", and quickly switch the focus to "you".

Summing up
All the way through your message, the reader wants to feel you're talking to him directly. That means using his style of language and his reference points to describe how you can help him. Just try seeing the world through his eyes.

If in doubt, try asking "So What?" every time you make a statement. It will force you to add a benefit to every feature, offer or promise...so the reader knows the answer to "What's In It For Me?"

AT A GLANCE

- ✓ Every feature should deliver at least one practical benefit
- ✓ Get specific with details like numbers, benefits, dates and deadlines
- ✓ Get to the point early - attention is a fickle mistress
- ✓ Use the reader's frame of reference - not yours
- ✓ Test your customer focus score with an online "we we" calculator
- ✓ Even "about" pages need customer focus

Talk about you and I'll switch off in a second. Talk about me and I'm there for the day!

PART 3
TAKING SHAPE

"Form follows function - that has been misunderstood. Form and function should be one, joined in a spiritual union."

Frank Lloyd Wright

– 10 –
Sales letter structures
*Non-pushy ways to write
and fill your order book*

"Sell me this pen," said the interviewer.

"Sell it to you?" queries 18 year old me. "Um, yeah ok..."

Some nervous fumbling as I checked out the half-eaten biro. Then finally:

"Look, it's a nice pen, isn't it? Just one careful owner. And see, it's got all the things, er, features you'd expect. Like the ink goes in here, so it flows through to the nib, that's handy. And when you're not writing you can put this cap on it so the ink doesn't go all over your fingers. Um...do you want one?"

"No."

"Why not?"

I'll spare you the rest, because the whole interview went downhill from there. I'll just cut to the end, where my never-to-be boss gave me my first lesson in sales.

You guessed right: I should have opened with "What kind of pen are you looking for?"

Now I'm sure you've had a similar interview (although I doubt you messed it up as spectacularly as I did). But for me, it was an hour well spent - because that one lesson is the basis of every sale I've ever made, in person and in print.

The lesson being, get to the problem or aspiration first. Then the sale is just the solution.

OK, now you're probably saying "Well duh!", because that's truly basic stuff. But I still talk to sales people who don't think problem-solution...and I read a huge amount of copy that makes the same mistake.

So for a page or two, pardon me if I'm stating the obvious. But I'd like to cover all bases, just in case the 18-year-old me ever gets to read this.

The 5 things you need to make a sale

You can't get another human being to dip into his pocket and hand you the precious cash therein unless you can do the following:

1. Touch a raw nerve
2. Offer the antidote

3. Silence doubters
4. Inject some urgency
5. Give an instruction

So before you sit down and write your stunning sales piece, think where each element sits in your message.

Touch a raw nerve
We've said it already. Build your message around the pleasure or the pain. Think back to Chapter 7 and Phil's Insomnia Button...that big emotive thingy that's keeping him awake...and you've got a foundation ready-made.

"I can't afford my mortgage", "my computer is too slow", "I don't know how to tap-dance", "I'm hungry", "I'm cold" etc. The underlying problem or aspiration is always your starting point.

Offer the antidote
I'm guessing your business is geared up to solve the problem or fulfill the ambition? Great, but your message has to explain that, and make it clear why your solution is the pick of the bunch.

Silence doubters
When we find a solution, we want to believe it's true. But the sentry part of the brain yells out "Hang on, this could be dodgy!"...so you have

to help the reader to believe you're the genuine article, by adding things like examples, testimonials and guarantees.

Inject some urgency
Why should they do it now? Why not wait 'til tomorrow, or next year? Give a reason to act right away, like a limited supply or a short term offer or bonus. Or just the pain of coping without the solution for one day longer.

Give an instruction
It's been said that we're all walking round with an invisible umbilical cord, looking for somewhere to plug it in! So be explicit: how do they take action? Give specific guidance.

With all five elements in your message, you're on solid ground.

But take any one away, and you're in one deep pile of doggy doo.

Structuring the message
The five elements are like ingredients that go into a cake. But a simple list of ingredients is not much of a recipe - you also need a method statement, so you know how to mix it all in.

So now, we're going to look at ways to pull your message together.

We've already covered one useful option. Back in Chapter 7, we used *Problem-Agitate-Resolve* as a formula for developing a basic sales pitch.

The formula works, because it focuses the mind on pain and the need for an easy fix. And of course, it's easy for you to work all five elements into the message.

But it's not the only option. There are umpteen other ways to structure your sales message, and we're going to take a shufty at my two favourites here. We'll start with the standard-bearer:

AIDA

The classic motivating sequence follows the four steps that take a prospect from indifference to commitment:

Attention – Interest – Desire – Action

Debate rages over its origins, some crediting Elias St. Elmo Lewis, and others saying it belongs to A. F. Sheldon. The truth is probably somewhere inbetween, because it evolved over a number of years. But hey, that's academic. We should thank them both, because it works.

To show AIDA in action, here's a letter for a company that runs sports clubs during school holidays:

The holidays are coming
*And that means playtime.
Like it used to be...*

Dear [Parent or Guardian]

Like me, you probably spent your school holidays running here and there. Jumping. Playing. Breathing fresh air. It's what we did in the years before games consoles and 24-hour TV.

Well, at [Company Name] we want kids to have all the same chances today - to play safely in the sunshine and know the thrills of taking part in healthy, fun activities.

So this half-term, you'll find us at [venue], putting 4-12 year olds through their paces. For 5 hours a day, there's football, cricket, hockey, street dance, basketball... something for everyone.

It's a chance for kids to polish their skills, or try their hand at something new and exciting.

And don't worry: we're not elitist here. We offer a safe and friendly place where kids can develop through sport. So we don't care about ability - it's all about taking part, with every child doing the best they can.

Now…as you'd expect, these sessions are always popular, but as of today there are spaces. It's a chance for your child to get out and get active, make new friends and burn off some energy.

It beats watching cartoons all day…and the whole week is just £40 all in.

So please fill in the leaflet enclosed and hand it back into the school. That's all you need to do between now and the start of the holidays.

I'm looking forward to hearing from you - and sharing the joys of a healthy lifestyle.

Yours etc.

P.S. Our fully qualified coaches are trained in every vital discipline, from Health & Safety right through to Child Behaviour Management. So you can carry on with your day, knowing your child is safe *and* having a great time…

Just fill in the form today, and we'll do everything else.

This letter is short and simple, but it's been effective because it follows the AIDA flow:

Attention
The letter went out two weeks before the school holidays – a time when most parents are wondering how to keep their kids occupied. So the headline is a reminder that the holidays are coming, coupled with a teasing pledge to solve the problem.

Interest
In the sub-heading, there's a hint of nostalgia, with "playtime, like it used to be". Then the first paragraph builds on that, harking back to the parent's own childhood. This draws them into paragraph 2, which is all about empathy: the need to get kids out in the fresh air. So when the solution is described in paragraph 3, the reader has an emotive reason to focus on the problem.

Desire
The paragraph that starts "And don't worry" is all about easing concerns and killing misconceptions. This allows the reader to feel they're making a safe and wise decision - and once they feel that, their desire can take over.

At the end of the paragraph, we get the aspirational line, "every child doing the best they can" - a useful trigger for many parents of junior school kids.

Action
The next paragraph ("Now...as you'd expect") moves in for the sale. Straight away, there's a hint of scarcity, to suggest the parent should sign up early, together with a reminder of the main benefit.

Then in the next line, when the price is revealed, there's another emotive reason to act. No parent wants their child to be sat watching cartoons all day - so in that context, £40 for the whole week feels like a small investment.

The principle here is, cushion the blow of the price by showing the consequence of not taking action. In this example, the price is low anyway, but it's a very useful tactic when you've got the "sticker shock" of a high price.

Finally, there's an instruction set out in bold, so the parent knows what to do. It sounds effortless, and comes with the reassurance "That's all you need to do between now and the start of the holidays". It's making life easy.

Then after sign-off, there's a PS. Every sales letter should have one - either to re-state a main benefit or add something new that builds desire or boosts credibility.

That's it. That's AIDA.

I've chosen this example because it's gently persuasive. It manages to push the sale without straying from the conversational tone. There's no cheesy "Roll up, roll up, get it now!", and no aggressive "What are you waiting for?"…instead, it shows the reader some respect and still makes a compelling offer.

And most importantly, it did its job by filling thousands of places.

Take another look and see how it moves through the different stages of AIDA. And also note where the five elements fall naturally into the copy: how it touches the raw nerve, offers the antidote, silences doubters, injects some urgency and gives an instruction.

Could you rewrite it?
While the letter was effective, it's certainly not perfect. There are many other ways it could be written with the AIDA formula. Here are 10 examples:

1. The writer tells the story of why he set up the company - because his kids were hanging round the house all day playing video games.
2. The story of one child who went from zero to hero…and it all started with some fresh air and exercise.

3. Compare two kids of the same age, and how they're spending the holidays.
4. Describe an older child who's struggling with fitness, and how it could have been avoided. For younger kids, it's not too late...
5. Answer a common fitness question with an expert warning.
6. Describe a typical day's activities, to bring the experience to life.
7. Tackle misconceptions in detail, like a parent's worries over elitism.
8. Tell a story that shows why taking part is more important than winning.
9. Let the parent off the hook: you know they'd like to be at home with their kids, but in this economy everyone has to work long hours...
10. Tell the story of one child who came along reluctantly last time, and had the time of his life.

Try one of these angles - or one of your own - to test the AIDA formula and see how your natural voice comes through. It'll be half an hour well spent.

Moving on...

AIDA is the ultimate message structure, but there are others you can apply. If you're looking for an alternative, try this:

The 5Ps
You might know the 5Ps as a marketing system (Product, Price, Place, Promotion, People). But that's about developing a strategy. This is different.

The writing formula of the same name is a structure that's often credited to Robert W Bly, a legendary US Copywriter and author of "The Copywriter's Handbook". It stands for:

Picture – Promise – Product – Proof - Purchase

In other words, you describe the end result first, then flesh out the proposition.

In a nutshell, you'd be saying: "Imagine life like this...well thanks to xyz it could happen...this is the widget and why it's so great...and this is how you know it works...you can get it here". Or in a bit more detail:

Picture
Start off by describing how life is going to be- the "all is well", end of the rainbow stuff. Give the reader the sense that he's already holding the answer in his hands.

In our holiday sports club example, you might describe the child coming home on the final day, clutching a trophy or certificate and buzzing with excitement. He hasn't watched TV all week, because he's been too busy playing, taking part, making the most of his holiday.

Promise
Set the reader's expectations by making a solid promise. Now the benefit starts to feel real, as all kinds of questions start to form in his mind.

In our example: this is what happens when kids get a taste for healthy, organised activities. They have fun, make new friends and discover talents they didn't know they had.

Product
Describe the widget that makes it all possible, with some detail of features and benefits...all harking back to that feel-good factor that you promised at the start.

In our example: describe the holiday club and the games on offer...and how it often spurs kids into a long-term healthy lifestyle.

Proof
The reader's emotional side is hooked, but their rational side wants more. So silence the doubts by adding some proof, like credentials, guarantees or testimonials.

In our example: focus on the coaching team's qualifications and the importance of safety. You might also add in the lack of elitism here.

Purchase
Time to move in for the sale. As you do, it helps to refer back to the original picture, so the whole message hangs together.

In our example: give the price and booking instruction, reminding the reader that they'll be getting affordable childcare and the kids will have a week they'll never forget.

See how it works?

Summing up
So which structure is right for you?

AIDA works in just about any circumstance, so it's the default for most copywriters. It's easily adapted for any product or service - whether it's something you actively want, or just something you need.

The 5Ps is ideal for aspirational products, like home improvements, fitness equipment and luxury goods. It's also great for abstract products that rely on a feel good factor (like holidays, dining out, hot air balloon rides and more) because it "installs" the feeling in your mind and makes it seem real.

Problem-Agitate-Resolve works especially well for grudge purchases - things like insurance, dental care, health plans, loft insulation, wills and other things the customer needs but doesn't actually want.

There are other angles to choose from, but these three alone give you enough ammunition for every sales message you'll ever write.

AT A GLANCE

- ✓ Every message needs the basic ingredients: touch a raw nerve, offer the antidote, silence doubters, inject some urgency and give an instruction
- ✓ AIDA helps you to structure any kind of sales pitch...but don't ignore the other methods
- ✓ For grudge purchases like wills or insurance, try Problem-Agitate-Resolve
- ✓ For aspirational copy, try using The 5Ps
- ✓ Toy with different ways of making your point: tackle misconceptions, answer questions, make comparisons, or show how you've helped others

The right message is the right mix of structure, content and style. Take one away and the whole thing falls apart.

– 11 –
Sales letter pitfalls
A few caveats, before your letter hits the mat

Have you seen the film "Brewster's Millions"?

Richard Pryor plays a minor league baseball star who inherits a whopping sum - but first, he has to blow a cool $30 million in 30 days. He runs around trying this and that, and finds it an uphill struggle.

Someone should have told him: the easy way to go broke is to screw up a direct mail campaign!

Send the wrong letter to the wrong audience...make a few rookie mistakes...and you'll be broke in 48 hours flat.

If only he'd known sooner - he could have spent the rest of the film playing baseball.

So, before you put your sales letter together... or even a plain old email...I'm going to touch on a few last (but vital) considerations. Some points in this chapter stay inside our copywriting remit, but others step outside and into the wider realms of direct marketing. So you might say I'm going off script here and there, but I'm going to cover it anyway.

I don't want this book to be the reason you blew £10k on a mailshot!

Sitting comfortably? Let's begin...

Never sell to a stranger
I'm guessing that your parents told you, never talk to strangers. Well now, I'm begging you: don't try to sell them anything either!

They don't know or like or trust you yet...so why should they buy from you? Yet time and again, I see people sending sales letters to a cold - and unqualified - list. Then they wonder why it's bombed.

It's like saying hello to some random person you've just met at the bus stop, then wondering why they didn't invite you round their house for tea and crumpets.

Insane.

Two basic truths apply here: for someone to respond to your message, they have to know you - and they have to want or need your type of widget. So before you start, I'd urge you to take a long hard look at your list. Does every person deserve their place?

Some definitions might help here.

By "know you", I mean they have some kind of relationship with your business. Either they've bought from you before, or they've made an enquiry, or they've given you express permission to contact them. That doesn't mean they handed you a business card at some networking bash or trade show...it means they've stated explicitly that they want your marketing messages, or they've given you their details in order to grab some kind of freebie.

"Want or need your type of widget"? Well, there are different levels of want and need, but you should have some reason to believe your widget could light up their world. That could mean:

- They have a relevant job, business, hobby or interest
- They've bought (or explored) a widget like yours in the past
- They're at a stage in life (like graduation, marriage, parenthood or retirement) where your widget is relevant

Plus, whatever their reason for buying, you need a strong indication that they can afford said widget. Either because of their demographic, credit score or their type of job or business.

So what's the upshot of this?

In email terms, it means never, ever buy a cold list. If recipients don't know you, you're just another spammer - and that can stop your emails getting through to genuine prospects.

And in direct mail (or "junk mail") terms, it means take one step at a time. If you don't have a list of suitable prospects who know you, build one from scratch. Offer them something free first, to get the relationship going...then sell to the people who raise their hand. Everyone else falls by the wayside.

Here are three ways to grow a list:

Starting online:
When someone comes to your website, capture their email address by offering your something of value - say a free report or video that helps them to solve a problem.

Keep sending them useful info, then offer to send them something even more useful. But this time, it's a physical widget, so it has to go through the post...and you'll send it either free of charge or for a nominal fee.

Now they know you. You know their interests. And you've got their contact details...so you can move in for the sale, using a mix of letters and emails.

Starting with adverts:
Use online and offline advertising to start a second list. One way is to use press ads to offer your free report or widget - then send it to responders, and follow up with the sales message. By choosing the right type of media, you can improve the quality of responses. For example, if you're a house builder selling starter homes, you might get a good response by advertising in bridal magazines.

Another option is to advertise through Facebook or LinkedIn, and use their targeting tools to make sure your ad is only seen by the right people. Staying with the starter homes example, you can seek out newly-weds and people who've just got engaged, and show them one kind of ad. Then you can create a separate ad for another group of relevant prospects - maybe people who graduated in the last 2 years, because chances are they're about to get on the property ladder.

Starting with a mailer:
Buy a list of suitable people who you can nurture over time. Any good list broker will have access to data from publications, surveys and other mailshots, so they can help you find people in the right category.

They can also drill down further so you target according to behaviour. And that means:

- Instead of just mailing everyone with an active interest, you can focus on people with an actual buying habit
- Or refine again, so you've only got people who've bought many times over…
- Or refine again, so you've only got people who've bought from multiple brands…
- Or refine again, so you've only got people who've bought through direct mail…
- Or refine again, so you've only got people who are due to renew or upgrade

In all these examples, the key point is that you're not selling straight away. You start the relationship by giving...and giving to the right kind of person…so when the time comes to sell, the prospect is already in your fan club.

Of course, it means you're spending money just to get a list of prospects – no actual sales yet. But remember, it means you're going to spend less on long-term mailing, because now you're closer to finding the needles in the haystack.

That should make the investment less painful. But if not, there's a second way to ease the cost burden: just create a low cost entry level product, to offer as a follow-up to your freebie. It could be something as simple as a printed – or expanded - version of your free report. If you charge a few shekels, a percentage of responders will pay the upgrade. And that should recoup your ad or mailing costs...as well as giving you a list of hyper prospects who are ready to spend with you right away.

One letter good, five letters better

As I'm sure you've heard, very few sales are made at the first attempt. You've probably seen the stats that say 80% of business comes from relentless follow-up. That's why experts recommend 5 or more messages in a mailing sequence.

It makes sense. First because it takes time for an offer to get noticed and sink in, and secondly because you can't say everything in one single message.

Chances are, there are many different reasons people buy from you...lots of insomnia buttons...and they all have to be addressed.

If you're selling cars, the buttons could be freedom, economy, comfort, style or prestige - and no matter how well you profile your list, you can't be certain that you know the right button to push for every prospect.

So send five letters, and focus each one on a particular theme. Then at some point in the sequence, every reader gets at least one highly relevant message.

And if you want to get really smart, use the data you have on each customer to pre-suppose their personal buttons - then mail the letters in order of relevance. Once they respond, you can stop mailing, so your costs come down...again.

Another way to build a mailing sequence is to scoop up early responders with a simple postcard, then send a more detailed letter or two to the non-responders. Finally, send a shorter letter to mop up the procrastinators. If you can, send emails inbetween, with a link to a sales landing page.

And don't be afraid to pick up the phone. It's hard work, but you should be making life easier for the customer...not yourself!

Don't sell in an email
Door to door sales people know how to make a pitch on the doorstep. They'll tell you just enough to tease...but they'll wait 'til you invite them in before giving the full presentation.

Have you ever wondered why?

It's not because they want to have a nice sit down and a cup of tea. It's because they know, out on the doorstep, they're just an unwelcome intruder.

But once they're inside, you've given them permission to carry on. You'll be more receptive to their message, because now you've said "Yes, let's hear it".

It's the same in an email.

Like the guy stood out on the doorstep, the email is an intruder. It's cutting through all the other stuff you're trying to deal with. And the only way around that is to get "over the threshold".

Or in email terms, get the reader to click through to a landing page.

Now they're receptive. Now you can sell.

The email is just the tease – so you're not selling the product, you're just selling the need to find out more. But that doesn't mean your email has to be short and snappy. The ideal length is whatever it takes to pique the reader's interest - so toy with a mix of long and short emails and see where you get the response.

Don't preach to the choir
Staying with our friendly door to door sales guy, you've probably noticed his job is a wee bit harder than the bloke who works in the showroom. Out on the door, he's got to break down your resistance. While in the showroom, a simple "How can I help?" can lead to a big fat order.

If the showroom bloke took the doorstep approach, he'd be just a bit full-on. The people he's talking to have already expressed an interest, so there's no need to sell too hard. Just show the solution - job done.

In copy terms, this is the difference between a sales letter and a product or service page on your website.

A sales letter (or a sales landing page that's triggered by an email) is a full-on sales piece – the written equivalent of our man on the door. But a product or service page is just the bloke in the showroom.

In practical terms, that means your product and service pages don't have to batter the reader into submission. Instead of describing the sheer agony of living without the solution, give a quick reminder of the pleasure or pain…just to add context and build some empathy...then get on with showing that you've got the thingamajig, whatever it is.

Better still, show that you've got the solution and then some. Focus on the limitations of the standard version, and sell the benefits of the super deluxe.

If that feels risky, test one version against the other and let the market decide.

One offer, but lots of options
Blinkered horses win races, because they can't see all the stuff that's going on around them. Their gaze is narrowed and fixed on the end result. Customers are much the same.

Give a customer or prospect too many choices and they'll get distracted. So keep them focused on one thing and one thing only. One product or service, one offer, one deadline.

The only time to offer choice is when it comes to response. Then it pays to give them as much choice as you can...like two or three payment options, and a choice of responding by email, phone, web, text or old-fashioned coupon.

Yes, coupons still work! Especially with the older generation. And because they involve some effort – cutting out, filling in, posting –

they tend to give you more motivated, better qualified prospects.

Segmentation rules
Everyone is different. But we're not as different as we think. We share lots of our quirks and characteristics with others, like our interests, our values, our style of language...so it makes sense to group certain types of customers together. Send one message to one group, send another to the next.

Segmentation is a massive topic and there's no space to cover it in real detail here. But in principle, it means finding the common factors between the customers in your database. Do they all live in similar areas, or all work in the same type of business, or all fall into the same income bracket?

What unites them, and what separates them from the other groups in your list?

If you're selling B2c, you could start with demographics. A company like Experian can help you sort your database into segments and give you all kinds of insights into each group's behaviour. Just by knowing which newspaper they're likely to read, or where they're likely to shop, you can make strong assumptions about their values and style of language.

Sun readers and Telegraph readers will be open to very different messages!

Selling B2b? You can use Sic codes to put companies into pigeon holes, and use credit scoring systems to group again according to turnover. You can also apply your own instinct by checking company websites. If their style is gently professional, give them something simple and chatty...and if their style is more off-the-wall, get into their spirit and take some liberties!

You can also couple segmentation with a hint of personalisation. Drop fields into your copy where the mailing system inserts variable data, like someone's name or line of business or other info you've got on file.

The smartest companies use segmentation and personalisation to the nth degree, to the point where they're almost talking to each person on a one-to-one basis.

That's rarely doable for a smaller business, at least in the early stages, but some broad segmentation should be easy.

Just talk to a list broker and/or database manager...it's worth the time, money and effort.

Split testing never ends
There's a perfect version of every message, somewhere out there in the ether. The only problem is finding it…and recognising its value when you see it! So every campaign should include some systematic trial and error.

Let's say you write a sales letter and mail it to 2000 people. You get 20 responses, so you call that 1%. Not bad…but how do you take it further, to get 1.5% and more?

At that point, your only option is guesswork, because you don't know which bits of your letter really hit home with the readers, and which bits let you down.

So instead of one letter going out to 2000 people, you create two letters and send each one to 1000 people. The second letter is almost identical to the first, but one thing is different – maybe a different headline, layout, offer, deadline, level of detail etc.

Then you apply a tracking system, like using different phone numbers, web addresses or offer codes for each letter - so you know which version has generated the most responses at the end.

Next:

- If neither letter works, it's back to the drawing board. Try getting some expert advice before you mail again.
- If both work, but there's no clear winner, run the test again until you can be sure which version is most reliable. You might try increasing the size of your list this time round, or running the test 2 or 3 times. Does a pattern start to emerge?
- If one out-performs the other by a significant margin, you have a winner. That becomes your control...and your next test letter goes head to head with it, trying to take its place.
- Every time you mail, try a new test against your current control. One variation at a time, so you can pinpoint the reason for success or failure. And don't forget the lessons you've learned from your previous tests.

Long or short copy?
For years, copywriters have debated, is long copy more effective than short copy? And the whole debate misses the point. It's not about writing a long letter for the sake of being long...it's about saying everything that needs to be said, no matter how short or how long.

If you can say everything you need to say in the space of 200 words, then 201 words is too long. But if a 10,000 word letter leaves questions unanswered, then 10,000 words is too short.

It's really that simple.

Still, people argue that no-one will read a super-long message. And that's a mistake.

If someone wrote you a 50-page letter, with your name at the top in a headline that says "I know all your dirty secrets", you'd want to read the whole thing. You might only scan it, or you might read it from end to end...that depends on your personal nature...but one way or another, you'll want to know exactly what's being said.

The point being, if your message gets under the reader's skin, they'll stay with it regardless of length. Scan it or read it, they'll want all the detail.

So don't be afraid of long copy. But also bear in mind, length reflects commitment. The more you want from the reader, the more information they'll expect.

For example:

- If you're just capturing leads, you don't need chapter and verse - just enough to persuade the reader to hand over some contact details. They'll part with an email address more readily than a postal address, and need more persuasion again to give you a contact number.
- If you're asking them to call to enquire, they'll need far more detail. They won't pick up the phone until they're already committed to the idea of doing business...so your copy will have to do most of the selling. But not all of it.
- If you're selling direct from the page, you'll need to go into full detail. Answer every possible question, handle every objection and give them every possible reason to take action, and do it now.
- The more expensive the item, the more you'll need to inform. A book that sells for £8.99 won't need as much copy as a car that sells for £100k.

You'll also find that ideal length varies between B2b and B2c. In business, people - especially senior people - have less time and make faster decisions. So while you don't have to keep it short, you should get to the point straight away and keep it ultra-concise.

Marmite is fine
A client once asked me to take out a remark, "because it might cause offence". I asked if customers would be offended. He said no, but others would be.

So what??

If you worry that your message will alienate or offend some group or other, you'll end up with a neutral, vanilla pitch that doesn't provoke any kind of response - positive or negative.

This is a massive problem for some large corporations and public bodies. They don't want to feed the trolls in forums and discussion groups, so they sacrifice sales. It makes no sense.

My advice: create a message for potential buyers - everyone else is irrelevant.

Beware the evil 2% myth
I don't know where it came from, but this crazy rumour has wormed its way into the public conscience. It says "If you send out a mailshot, you should expect a 2% conversion".

Total, utter horseshit.

Just take these two scenarios:

Scenario #1: you run a local pizza delivery service, and you keep a database of all your best customers – the people who buy from you at least twice a month. On the day that England are playing in the World Cup Final (well, it could happen), they all get a personalised letter from you announcing a footie-themed offer.

Maybe you've named a special edition pizza after one of the star players, or some garlic bread after the goalie...whatever. Point is, you make an incredible offer, brimming with a sense of occasion, designed for anyone holding a world cup party. But it's for this one big night only.

Mid-afternoon, you back up the offer with an email...then an hour before kick-off, everyone gets a second email plus a reminder by text. At half time, there's one last text, making reference to the score and state of play, and pledging to get the pizza there before the final whistle blows.

Likely conversion? It could easily hit 20 or 30%. Maybe more.

Now, scenario #2: you're selling top of the range helicopters. They're truly awesome machines, worth several million squid apiece. And you're sending a generic letter to everyone on the electoral roll.

Likely conversion? There's not enough paper to print all the zeroes that fall after the decimal point, but if you're lucky you might sell one for every 10 million letters mailed.

Where does 2% fit in there?

I can't stress this enough, because it's becoming one of the most dangerous figures in direct marketing.

The fact is, there's only one way to measure the success of any campaign. It's not to put a finger in the wind and suppose, or to follow the 2% myth. It's return on investment. Nothing more.

If it makes you money, it's a success. If it makes you more money, it's a bigger success. And if it costs you money, it's a failure.

Just one caveat though: if you're selling to prospects, you're creating new customers who'll buy from you time and again. So ROI is about the lifetime value of the customer – not just the value of the first sale.

This is a hugely important point…so worth a bit of expansion.

First, you have to gauge what an average customer is worth to you over time. For example, if you're a hairdresser, a new customer might come to you 6 times a year for a £50 hair-do. So they're worth £300 a year, and stay with you for an average of 3 years. That makes the customer lifetime value £900.

Therefore, if your campaign costs you £1800, you need 2 customers just to break even.

Then you set a higher figure – let's say 10 customers – and decide if you hit that number, it's been worth the risk and effort. If you can say you earned £5 for every £1 you spent, you know you've got a winning formula that you can repeat time and again.

But imagine if you only looked at the immediate return.

Suddenly, 2 customers at £50 each equals £100, against an up-front spend of £1800. Even 10 customers only gives you £500 first time out…so unless you look at the bigger picture, you're going to think it's unprofitable.

And it's not.

I know, there are issues like cashflow and different customers with different habits, so obviously you have to plug in your own numbers first. But the principle stands: if you know the lifetime value of a new customer, you can invest a decent amount of money to bring them in.

Summing up
Structure is only the start of your direct sales campaign. There are principles of direct marketing that have to go hand in hand with any written piece. We've only covered some of the fundamentals here, but follow these and you'll have far more success…whether you're writing a sales letter, email series or sales landing page.

Overall the message is, do everything you can to avoid the hard sell. Grow the relationship with the customer by holding a relevant conversation and sharing something of value–then one of two great things will happen:

Either they raise a hand and approach you – which gives you the upper hand in any negotiation.

Or (worst case) they're on your side by the time your sales message hits.

They know you're the real deal now…so assuming they're ready to buy, why would they choose anyone else?

AT A GLANCE

- ✓ Never sell to a stranger: they don't know, like or trust you yet
- ✓ Build a list using your website, direct mail and a mix of online and offline ads
- ✓ A single message rarely works – follow-up is essential, using lots of different channels
- ✓ Don't sell in an email, because you're still in "intruder mode"
- ✓ Don't preach to the choir: if the reader's half-sold, confirm the need and sell the solution
- ✓ Stick to one offer, but offer at least 2 or 3 ways to respond
- ✓ Use segmentation: different people respond to different messages
- ✓ Split test every message until you find the most effective version…then carry on testing
- ✓ It's not about long or short copy, it's about making your point
- ✓ Be as "Marmite" as you have to be…your message is for genuine prospects only
- ✓ Beware the 2% myth: the only measure is ROI, and that's in terms of lifetime value

Direct Marketing can turn a pauper into a millionaire…but it also works the other way round. Beware the pitfalls!

– 12 –
Writing to inform
*Staying on the radar
with regular content*

The lesson from the last chapter is that selling is easier if you take the time to educate the customer first.

So in this final chapter, we're going to look at helpful, informative copy: what it is, where to use it and how to write it.

First, let's take a peek at the content matrix and where your helpful messages will slot in…

The content matrix
There's no definitive list, because content that works for some won't necessarily work for others. If you sell to octogenarians, you won't get too much business through Twitter. If you sell to teens, forget LinkedIn.

It's all about the audience.

Broadly speaking, your content matrix is made up of four categories:

Category #1:
Content on your website...including:
- Home page
- About page
- Product & service pages
- FAQs
- Sales landing pages
- Squeeze (opt-in) pages
- Case studies
- Portfolio pages
- Infographics
- Articles
- Videos
- Podcasts
- Free reports / white papers
- Contact / enquiry pages

Category #2:
"Catch-all" web content...including:
- Your blog
- LinkedIn page
- Facebook page
- YouTube channel
- Twitter feed
- Syndicated press releases
- Google Maps listing
- Open discussion groups
- Profiles and content on sharing sites (videos, articles, images, presentations etc)

Category #3:
Targeted web content...including:
- Auto-responder emails
- Ongoing emails / e-zines
- Webinars
- Search ads, e.g. Google, Bing or Yahoo
- Banner ads e.g. LinkedIn, Facebook or Google Remarketing
- Closed discussion groups
- Password-protected profiles and content, e.g. on membership sites

Category #4:
Offline content...including:
- Sales letters
- Customer letters: consolidation, upsell, loyalty and retention
- Postcards
- Brochures
- Leaflets, flyers and handouts
- Editorials and advertorials
- Free and subscription newsletters
- Business cards
- Press ads
- TV or radio ads
- Billboards

As you can see, there's a time to advertise or sell...but a huge percentage of the matrix is best defined as factual, helpful and informative.

On your website, you've got articles, videos, podcasts etc, all designed to make someone's day and position you as the big fishy in your pond.

Around the web, you've got blogs, social media posts, more articles, more videos, all pointing back to your site. All great for positioning (and SEO).

Then offline, even print media shies away from the big sale sometimes. Newsletters, press coverage, loyalty messages…it's all info-led, designed to build awareness and good will.

So what does it all mean to you?

Your customers associate you with one part of their lives. So help them to improve it, by sharing any advice you can.

Example: let's say you're a greengrocer, so customers associate you with healthy eating. Here are three approaches you can take:

Approach #1: ways to use you more often
Give them healthy recipes using the latest season's ingredients- maybe through an online newsletter, a video series, a free booklet or a tip sheet. You can't lose here, because you're earning good will and it gives the customer lots of reasons to buy more from you.

But that's only the start.

Approach #2: remove the obstacles
If you look at the barriers to healthy eating, you'll find more content ideas. Like these:

Obstacle: people struggle to find the time to prepare healthy meals.

Solution: give them 5 minute recipes, or tips on how to find time for cooking at the end of a busy day.

Obstacle: parents can't get their kids to eat their greens. They just want Macdonald's!

Solution: give them a recipe for home-made burgers with healthy side dishes…plus a few tips on how to get the kids to eat their greens. (You could even buddy up with the butcher next door: you promote him to your list, he promotes you to his).

Obstacle: healthy food is dull and tasteless…the stuff that's bad for you is so much nicer!

Solution: give them recipes that use a touch of the tasty stuff in calorie-controlled portions. Or give them a calorie counter so they can eat the odd naughty thing without feeling guilty.

That gives you more to write about. And there's a third, final angle you can use that might feel suicidal at first...but don't dismiss it out of hand:

Approach #3: help them live without you
Give out tips on how to grow your own fruit and veg...how to manage your allotment, treat the soil, compete in summer fetes for the best marrow prize...all that stuff.

I know it sounds crazy, but it won't be bad for business. Here's why:

Most people who read it are in *some day never* mode: they read with good intent, thinking it's something they'll do some day. But they never get round to it. And in the meantime, they can see you're a genuine, honest and helpful supplier.

Meanwhile, the few who read it and do something with it will become your biggest fans. They'll recommend you to all and sundry, and they'll still need you themselves – either because they fail and decide they're better off coming to you, or because they can't do it all on their own. They've got lovely marrows, but what about turnips?

This third approach applies to any business where the layman can "have a go". I'm not suggesting that butchers give tips on slaughtering cows in the garden shed, or that surgeons tell you how to perform your very own lobotomy…but if it's learnable, help them do it. The numbers will stack in your favour.

So – think about your customers and where you slot into their lives. Then offer some help on that subject. In practice that could mean:

- Electricians talk about gadgets and gizmos, or renovating rooms
- Dentists give tips on meeting people and presenting yourself with confidence
- Plumbers give tips on lagging pipes, saving water and changing washers
- Beauticians give tips on fashion and preparing for dates or interviews
- Builders give tips on finding a plot or making better use of space
- Accountants talk about how to spend the upcoming tax rebate
- Printers give tips on marketing or how to source a reliable desktop printer
- Caterers give tips on event management
- IT people give tips on working from home, cyber security and choosing the best software

You get the idea. It all adds value, and reinforces the message "I'm here to help when you need me".

And it works. Personally, I can attribute over 50% of my copywriting business to articles I've written for my free newsletter. Even today, every time I hit "send", the phone starts ringing - and yet, there's no call to action in sight. It's selling, without actually selling.

OK, so how do you do it?
Articles, blog posts etc. take on all forms. But I'd say 90-ish per cent of successful pieces use one of these angles:

1. Offer "7 Easy Ways" to achieve something
2. Offer a single but detailed tip on the theme of "How To"
3. Tell a personal story and draw a lesson from it
4. Find something that's often overlooked, and champion its cause
5. Find something that's changed for the better, and urge the reader to think again
6. Reveal the hidden dangers of a popular tactic or habit
7. Share one secret that can save the reader time or money
8. List common mistakes or pitfalls, and how to avoid them

9. Look at underhand practices in your sector: has the reader been misled?
10. Introduce or analyse the latest phenomenon to hit your market
11. Help the reader to make sense of the latest trend in your market
12. Write a review of the latest product in your industry
13. Give a "warts and all" opinion on a current topic
14. Interview a notable person in your field, and share their insights
15. Tie into a recent news item, sports event or celebrity story
16. Tie into the latest hot debate, from news or popular culture
17. Write a "mailbag", answering reader's questions
18. Write about a customer or client, and what your widget has done for them
19. Look at what happened 5, 10, or 20 years ago and reflect on how times have changed
20. Write a round-up of everything that's going on in the industry

Once you've got an angle that works for you, writing the article is easy. For illustration, let's take angle #1, the "7 Easy Ways" to achieve something.

Of course, it doesn't have to be 7 ways, it could be any number you like. Curiously though, 7 seems to work better than other numbers - probably because it's a *Goldilocks* figure, between not enough and too much.

Structurally your article will look something like this:

HEADLINE - open with a question or statement that grabs the reader's attention. A simple "How To" works well for this type of article. Or as we've already covered, try making an obscure statement that hints at what lies ahead.

INTRODUCTION - set out your stall: why is this topic important, and how will you benefit from reading on?

MAIN CONTENT - in this case, that'll be the tips themselves.

CONCLUSION - end with a short epilogue. Maybe a summary or some inspiring words as a sign-off.

Trail it, tell it, and recap.

This structure is sometimes called the "News At 10" approach: start with the bongs, then the main news and sum up with a quick "and finally". In other words, tell them what you're going to tell them...tell them...then tell them what you've told them.

Here's an example article I wrote a few years ago for my newsletter. It's not Pulitzer Prize stuff (and it's got 12 tips, not 7). But hey, it did the job...

Are you using video on your website?

OK, I'm calling the kettle black here! I've been so busy revamping clients' websites that my own site is still sadly devoid of funky footage (for now). So yes, I'm the cobbler whose kids run around in the oldest pair of shoes!!

So get ahead of me (and more importantly, your competition) with these 12 top video tips for bringing your site out of the dark ages:

1. Grab a camera and do it! You don't have to be Spielberg. Just point it and talk...the web's not all HDTV!

2. Be helpful. Don't stare into the camera telling the world how great you are. Give

us your wisdom, not your sales pitch...then we'll decide for ourselves that you're awesome!

3. Keep it short. For the sake of bandwidth and diminishing attention spans, a series of 10x3 minutes is way, way better than 1 x30.

4. Answer your FAQs. Jot down your 10 most common questions - not the introspective stuff like "what time are you open?" and "how much do you charge?" - go for questions that will help customers get the most from your product or service.

5. Answer the questions people SHOULD ask! One video each - is that 10 more?

6. Add each video to YouTube with a different keyword on each. Then link each video to a relevant page of your website, using that page's target keyword as your anchor text.

7. Set up a YouTube channel, linking all your videos together. Let people subscribe to your feed so they'll know when you post something new.

8. Share your videos across the web, maybe using a paid distribution service like Traffic Geyser - always directing viewers back to your main website or blog.

9. Video your blog posts and cross-feed between your blog and YouTube so followers of each are totally in the loop.

10. Create a longer video - up to 10 minutes - for subscribers only. This is where you share some real pearls of wisdom. Then record a trailer for this video and add it to your homepage, asking visitors for their email address in exchange for the priceless info.

11. At the end of your 10-minute video, go nuts! You've finally earned a platform for self-promotion, so plug away. This is your moment!

12. Not everyone wants to watch a video. Slow connections are a nightmare, and some people would rather skim through text than let you dictate the pace. So put the gist of the message in text below the video...but don't transpose the whole video script. Make it the poor man's version so readers are compelled to go back and watch!

There you go - a quickie guide to getting started. I'll be taking all this to heart in the next few months, and hope you will too.

> Just one final thought: you have to stand out on YouTube, so the still image is all important. If it's you standing in front of the camera, you won't get many clicks. So make it as visual as you can. There's no point in doing it otherwise.
>
> OK, 'nuff said for one day. Let's get out there, and let's make movies...

Like I said, not prize material! But it worked, because it's chatty and informative. When you write an article, you might be tempted to sound like your favourite journalist, but please take my word here, you have to resist that urge at all costs. Journos have to sound neutral, so their language is dry and functional. That's fine if you're writing a press release, but an online article - and especially a blog post - should come from the natural you.

What about other factual copy?
Once you can write a decent blog or article, you've got skills you can adapt to all kinds of media. Here are some examples:

White Paper Reports
A white paper is just an extended article - usually given away on a website in exchange for the visitor's email address. The ideal angle is the second on our article list: offer a single

but detailed tip on the theme of "How To".

Just bear in mind, the word "single" is all important here. You don't want to be the headless chicken, running around aimlessly - keep it tight and focused. Help them to solve one problem, and solve it well...then leave everything else in reserve.

Generally, the most successful white papers offer fast and easy answers. The web has made us an impatient bunch who expect something for nothing, so "big problem, easy pay off" is a kind of sweet spot.

A great example would be:

> How to drop a dress size in 2 weeks, without going on a crash diet

There's a big emotive need there, the benefit is quickly available, and you can do it all without the usual pain and suffering.

Of course, your tips have to back it up! Otherwise, you'll lose face immediately and the customer will leave your list.

Game over.

Emails
A daily, weekly or monthly email offering some advice is much the same as an article - but you know it's going straight to a loyal audience, so you can develop a series of connected messages on one theme.

Emails are great for on-going lead generation. Once someone joins your list, they get regular emails from you. Each one offers some value and makes a not-too-forceful pitch at the end.

For inspiration, try any of the 20 angles above for articles and blog posts.

Videos
A helpful video will often go down better than the written word. Most of us would sooner watch the film than read the book, so a vid is an effortless way to gain some valuable info.

As mentioned in the sample article above, a lone piece to camera can be a little dull. So toy with different ways of getting your message across.

There are some great (and affordable) animation tools online, so you can create and voice your own characters, or create instant drawings that grab the eye. Or if you prefer, go less hi-tech - use sock puppets or your kid's toys to narrate on your behalf.

If it grabs attention, why not?

Webinars
Like a white paper, a webinar usually goes into real detail to solve a single problem. But instead of text, it's typically a narrated presentation, maybe with Q&As or a one-time offer at the end.

Structurally, the basic principles of writing articles apply: trail it, tell it and recap.

Podcasts & audio recordings
A podcast (or a CD) is just an audio tipsheet. It's just you, a microphone and some handy advice - or maybe an interview with an expert in your field. Either way, it stands to reason that the same chatty style is needed.

Often, you can go into even more detail in a podcast, because people will listen to them on the move. Sat at their desk, they're impatient and dipping in and out to check email or Facebook. But if they're locked away on a train, or in their car, they'll give you more attention. Exploit it!

Social Media Posts
Every tweet and Facebook update has to be written - and again, same rules apply. You'll get more likes and retweets when you talk about the customer, so remember The You

Factor every time you post. Try a mix of our headline types – self-interest, curiosity and revelation – and see what works for you.

In my experience, social media has three things going for it:

1. It keeps you on the customer's radar in a non-intrusive way.

2. It trails your articles, webinars, podcasts etc, finding you a wider audience.

3. It gives you (limited) metrics, so you can see which type of content is well received.

That said, it's full of distractions, so the reader's attention is easily lost - especially on Facebook, because we're mostly there for pleasure, not business. So it's best to tempt the reader away from the social page, and onto your blog or website where you'll get their full attention.

And please, if the stats say it's not working, go do something else. Likes and Retweets and Google Circles are a long, long way from sales.

And finally...Press Releases
I've left this one 'til the end, because - as I mentioned earlier - the style will be a little different.

A press release needs to be factual, written in the same objective language that you see in a newspaper or hear on the news. So - just on this occasion - you should drop the personal touch. Any comment or opinion should be offered as a quotation.

However, press releases still follow one of our main principles: don't talk about yourself - talk about what matters to the reader. As an ex-journo, I've seen thousands of dire press releases, and they were all written as shameless self-promotion.

No editor or journalist will ever plug your business unless you give them a real story or useful information.

And the flip side...getting to know you
Throughout this book, I've been preaching the same few messages – one being "it's not about you, it's about the customer".

And that's true. Except to say that well, it isn't. Now and then.

You see, some customers will value the chance to get to know you better - especially if you're an individual (like a consultant or coach) with a strong following or reputation in your field.

They'll want to hear about your life, your family, your hobbies. They'll want to see you posing with your new baby or playing with the cat. They'll want to share in your problems, and be with you through all the highs and lows.

Basically, they'll want to feel they're a member of your gang.

This stems from our tribal urge to belong and connect with the folks we admire. And in the age of social media and reality TV, we expect to be able to access any part of someone's life.

Now you can ignore this altogether and keep things on a strictly business level. Many do. But I've seen hordes of successful people who invite their readers in - some connecting with all comers on Facebook, and others just telling personal stories in their daily emails.

Only you can decide if this approach is right for you. But if you adopt it, my advice is:

- Reserve the personal touch for the people who've made some commitment to you - just your customers or clients, and the people who opt into your list. Your messages to the general public can't scream "Me me me!"

- If you can, relate the personal stuff back to your line of business. That's easy for anyone who deals in business support, or self-help things like fitness or complimentary therapies. For butchers, bakers and candlestick makers though, it's more of a challenge. Suck it and see.

- Personal stories can be a good way to generate leads and clicks to landing pages. But when you get to the actual sales pitch, your ego takes a back seat. The moment they're thinking of spending money, the message is all about them.

Summing up
Factual, informative copy is the accidental salesman: it goes out into the world, making everyone's day that little bit better, with no conditions or obligations. And it pulls in business anyway.

Sometimes it pays back straight away, other times it takes a while. So while you can't rely on it as your only source of business, it's a vital part of the marketing mix. Use it well…and use it often, lest ye be forgotten.

AT A GLANCE

- ✓ Sharing advice is the best way to gain the reader's trust and build a relationship
- ✓ Remember the basic structure: trail it, tell it and recap
- ✓ Stay on track: keep content focused on one issue, even if you offer multiple tips
- ✓ The same basic rules apply to webinars, podcasts, videos, emails, white papers and social updates...but each medium has its own quirks that you can exploit
- ✓ Press releases should be more objective, but still focused on the needs of the reader
- ✓ Consider letting the reader into your world, by sharing stories about your life

Staying top of mind is like keeping a balloon in the air. You can't rely on a single nudge. You have to keep on nudging!

Final word: getting started

Everything we've covered is just an expansion of the basic principles – make it relevant, simple and chatty – but it's still a lot to take in when you're writing line by line.

If you keep pausing to double-check your style or choice of words, you'll never get the momentum you need.

It'll feel like running through treacle!

So my suggestion: go back to your practice message – the rough cut you've been working with since the start of chapter 1. Take another stab at it now, but don't worry about the finer points we've covered. Just rewrite it using nothing but instinct, to see how your voice has developed.

My guess is you'll see an improvement straight away: it should sound more like you and be more focused on the reader.

If you didn't write the practice message, it's a good time to do it now. Start with a headline, then dive in and write a few hundred words in free flow.

Just write something. Anything. Get it down on paper.

Why? Well, it's been said (way too many times) that the blank page is every writer's nemesis. So you need to charge into battle, holding your pen aloft, crying "Aaarrrgghhhhh!" until you've killed it (or at least dealt a fatal blow).

If you have to, write down the very first line that pops into your head, even if it truly sucks. It doesn't matter - no-one else is going to see it, and chances are it will start a train of thought that leads you to that elusive great headline or opening statement.

Then follow it through. Write the whole thing, long and rich, getting every point across. Don't worry about length, grammar or phrasing – all you want is something to work with.

If you're still finding it doesn't flow, you might need to change your way of working. Personally, I can't write a first draft on a PC – it has to be done in hard copy, with a gel pen, a highlighter and a blank (un-ruled) sheet of A4.

I'm sure a Psychiatrist would tell me it's a hang-up, but so what? It works for me.

It might be because the physical page gets my full attention. I'm staring down at the desk, not looking at the computer with all its tempting little distractions.

Or it might be because I can write a full draft, then make some improvements as I write it up. I find that as the message starts to take shape on screen, the final pieces fall into place – banishing all the niggles and doubts that were down there on the page.

I know that Time & Motion says my process is inefficient, because I have to write every page out twice. But I write faster this way, so I get to the end goal sooner.

But then again, that's just me. I know writers who can just sit at the keyboard and tap up a masterpiece. And others who use voice recognition – or a PA – so they can dictate the first draft.

I know some who plan the message in detail, using the steps we've covered, and some who just dive in and write on instinct (copywriting meets jazz).

I can't tell you which working method will be right for you. All I can say is, experiment.

You'll find out soon enough.

Got your first draft ready?

Great...now here's a checklist of the 10 most important points we've covered:

1. Have you grabbed the reader's attention with a compelling headline?
2. Does your copy match the language you'd use if you met the reader in person?
3. Are your sentences short, clear and unambiguous?
4. Are you using the simplest words available?
5. Have you followed a structure like Problem-Agitate-Resolve, AIDA or The 5Ps?
6. Is the copy focused on the reader's hopes, needs and desires?
7. Have you covered all the most important points, like questions and objections?
8. Does the whole message have a seamless, natural flow?
9. Does the reader have a reason to believe what you say?
10. Does the reader know exactly what to do next – and why?

Over time, you'll start to cover all these points without batting an eyelid. But in the early days, my advice is, keep this checklist close to hand. Then try writing something every day, just to stay in the groove. A quick email, blog post or article at the start of every day is a quick win marketing wise, and a great way to stay in the writing habit.

Good luck.

Go forth and scribble.

...And sell a shedload of widgets too.

NEED MORE EXAMPLES?

Apart from endlessly writing, the best way to learn is to read other successful bits of copy. Get used to the quirks and nuances, until they're second nature.

Even copy them out in long-hand until you train your brain to write the same way.

So I've put together an online resource - and as a thank-you for reading this book, I'm offering you free access.

Just go to this web page:
www.jamesthecopywriter.co.uk/talk
and follow the instructions

If you'd rather not go it alone...

I'm a jobbing copywriter, flitting from mailer to web page, email, brochure, press release and wotnot. I've written for large and small companies, beaten controls, hiked up conversion rates and won a Canmol Award from the Chartered Institute of Marketing in Wales.

I also run training courses, to guide people through the whole writing process in person.

So, trumpeting over, the point is this: maybe I can help you.

I say "maybe" because I work alone, and have to sleep now and then. Plus I'll only take on a client if I believe in their product or service - and if I can see exactly how my copy will repay their investment.

If you think I can help, check out my website: www.jamesthecopywriter.co.uk.

Or call my office during business hours on +44 (0)845 643 6261 and put in a request for a 1-2-1 phone call.

After that? Well, let's see where it takes us...

My Actions

That's it! You've finished the book...so what are you going to do now?

1. *Practice writing by posting a 5-star review on Amazon:-)*
2.
3.
4.
5.
6.
7.
8.
9.
10.